Agony

A poem of genocide

by Mark Huband

with illustrations
by Anna Steinberg

LIVE CANON

First Published in 2020
By Live Canon Poetry Ltd
www.livecanon.co.uk

978-1-909703-92-6

Agony: A poem of genocide

To the memory of Paul Celan

Poet

1920-1970

Dopo di allora, ad ora incerta
Since then, at an uncertain hour,
That agony returns:
And till my ghastly tale is told,
This heart within me burns.

Primo Levi, *The Survivor*

1: Akazu

Closer. Closer to Being. To be so close.
And there were those who be. And the others.
It went like this. A truck to collect trash.
A gutter snake-snaking a city slope,
two women dumped where it passed the church gate.
There is the Holy Family. Holy.
Nuns praise the children for their nice drawings.
Their drawings of the Holy Family.
10   All is calm. All is bright. It goes like this
in the red-brick nave, alter slung with clothes
catching stained-glass light. All is bright, all
is calm in the gutter where a man now lies
with the women. The street is empty
under hot storm clouds. That is how it went,
and the Colonel signed my *laissez-passer*,
stamped his name: Théoneste Bagasora.
You can go anywhere you like,[1] he said.
You're quite safe. No harm will come to you.
20   We shook hands. We shook hands. And he smiled.
And he smiled. There, in the *akazu*.
Akazu. Small house. Where the family lives.
The family, plotting their life of Being.
How to be all that others must not be.

How to be, free from all that must not be.
That is what it is to be what can be,
in the trash truck carrying out the trash,
its tailgate swinging to-and-fro.
Image. Image gone. Image. Image gone.
Arm. Hand. Leg. Arm. Hand. Leg. Heads. Blood. It drips
like rain from truck to gutter. Drips like rain.
It is not rain. It is not an image.
It does not rain. And there is no image.
A traffic light changes. Red. Amber. Green.
A tailgate is swinging to-and-fro.
You're quite safe. No harm will come to you.
You are safe. You are safe. You are quite safe,
there on the street where the traffic lights change,
where some are Being and some are the dead
and one is the ghost of all he once said.
This one is the ghost of all that was said
of the date, of time eaten from within
the place of present, past and future. All
is calm, all bright, white folks on that last flight
that drifts across late evening light
that 10th of April 1994.
Four days on, and this ghost had been before,
moving slight beyond Kigali's lore
of the Being and those who would become
what that Being had been for.
                    Death as life. A way of life,
told by some in their stories of escape
of how they fled to safety and were saved
by the colour of the flags they drape
at windows where the drowning ones now waved.
Move. *L'ecole Antoine de St-Exupéry.*
Move. Evacuees with teddy bears. Move

30

40

50

by the backroad through the shanty fields.
Halt. Hill road. Men sit. Women sit. The screams.
60 Sit. Plead. Gang beats them with clubs. The silence.
Children cling to teddy bears. Move. Pet dogs
whimper. Girl dragged along the backroad. Halt.
Girl dragged by her clothes. Girl stares into eyes.
Eyes meet. Machete sheen. Girl stares. Machete.
Eyes meet. Truck moves. Girl dragged. Dead lie face down.
Girl gone. Eyes gone. A teddy bear is saved.
The saved are watched as they pass village yards,
eyed by killers whose eyes are shards
that cut through skin, flesh, rags, hair, blade-clawed fists
70 to the place where Being deals its cards
and a clipboard man ticks names on lists.
                    Names. In time. In absence. Names on a list.
                    Known. Unknown. Say your name. To be the name
once given. A name on a list. That name,
which became the body that she became
in the blood mud yard by the shanty track
the righteous drive without looking back
onto the place where the eye-shards rage
deep inside the skin and the flesh and the rags,
80 onto the place where the mysteries blaze
amid flesh-fed flame and the myth of flags
                    that drape the walls of the *akazu*.
                    They dream there of a perfect silence,
when the tick-name lists have been neatly filed
and the names they were been neatly piled
in the shade of the road to Rwamagana.

*

You can go anywhere you like.
You're quite safe. No harm will come to you,
90   because you are not the living nor the dead.
You neither sleep nor wake. You are your words on
a page, unspoken as the senses caged
in the hollow of the carcass you sketch
into your story of the living and the dead
that is never told in the *akazu*,
where life is the death of those who must not be.
          Will not be.
          Cannot be
their Being of silent ecstasy
100   this family in the *akazu* now dream that life can be.
          It is there,
            where the rebel soldier is peddling fast
past the rotting pile beneath the trees
holding his nose as his glance is cast
at a million dead humanities,
             it is there
             that somebody made their dream come true,
             where somebody built their *akazu*
          in the forest, by the river, on the lakeside, in the hills,
110   where they dream to make utopia
          before the one they're killing kills.
So let us go then, a little further
along the road from Rwamagana
among the trees where dapple morning
smooths the forest floor to marble
soothes the shrouding leaves that shiver
in the whisper of a breeze
that shifts the grief of mourning trees
now stooping where they gather
120   to bury beneath their fibrous tears

the dead strewn at their feet.
                    So let us go then, to where the clearing in the wood
                    defies the reason life has borne
                    the burdens of millenia.
There is no reason why Rukara church
in shadows cast by pine and birch
is the animal too frail to nurse its wounds.
Here the people built the tomb
they shaped from dreams lived in the womb
130   the outcast hates for all it gives
to the daughter of the one who lives. Death
seems life's revenge for being,
where a tabby cat trots on broken glass
and death's truth speaks as we pass
beneath the pulpit. The harvest is in,
its agony carved in the grin
of the hollowed skull beneath the skeins of skin
that rot like silk across the yard,
where charcoal dust upon a face
140   is the ashen mark of death's embrace.
It is the living who tell their story here,
they who came and made their life from the dead
that are the stones and stains and forest scent.
The dead are the earth, the dust, this place now silent,
while the living are the invisible truth
whose story lies beneath that church roof
in the agonies this witness must imagine.

                              *

There is nothing to imagine. There is only what can be seen.
Here is all that can ever be,
150   where the vegetables hum with honey bees

and a bird calls loud from the forest trees.
I hid with my daughter among the bodies
they left behind after the gendarmes had come.
We hid there until they had gone.
I think they thought we were dead,
so they left us,[2] Therese Uwilingyamana said
as she walked by the church.
Agathe Nsengimira clung to the baby she saved when she fled:
There were so many of them, with their weapons.
They came during the day to my home.
They knew where the Tutsis lived, on top of the hill.
I ran with my baby, but my young boy was left behind.
I didn't see him. He was running, but I lost him.
I could see them killing the people near the houses.
But I lost my boy.[3]

And our road passes into silence.

AT GATARE THE KARIBU BAR HAS BEEN DESTROYED. AT KIVEHE AN OLD MAN LIES DEAD ON THE ROADSIDE. AT NYAKAVAMBI DOGS ARE ROOTING AMONG THE TRASH. AT RWANTERU A FRIGHTENED BOY WANDERS ALONE. OUTSIDE KAYANZI, ABANDONED CATTLE CHEW GRASS, BAGS, POTS, BUCKETS, SHOES, PINEAPPLES, SACKS OF RIPE MAIZE AROUND ABANDONED FIRES. AT RUSUMO, FLEEING KILLERS HAD LEFT THEIR WEAPONS HEAPED BESIDE THE ROAD: MACHETES, KNIVES, DAGGERS, KITCHEN UTENSILS, HACKSAWS AND SPEARS, SOME STILL STAINED WITH BLOOD. BENEATH THE BRIDGE ACROSS THE KAGERA RIVER BORDER ANOTHER BODY PLUNGED DOWN RUSUMO FALLS.

Falling

to the whirlpool fury of the water.

Falling

tangled with the dead in the weed below.

Falling
                              through the living breathing life of the land
in the gaze of this witness where he stands
as the bridge between Being and its end,
a note on a page a truth he can't send,
of the Being that people cannot be
190   of lives that are not existence
of death that is not the end of life,
of a place where to kill is to live
where to kill is to save that life
where to kill is to be
not one of the fallen
tangled with the dead in the fury of water,
but among the living across the bridge
saved by death at the water's edge.
There they are, being the truth of what men do
200   beneath the shelter of the *akazu*,
where the lie of life and the truth of death
are sweat on a brow and the stench of breath.
                              Breathe. The forest once breathed
                              the rise and heave of the slopes that weave
                              with the light and silver of the eastern lakes,
                              where there was the rumour of a happening,
                              spread by voices heard
                              among the whispers and the pleas.
Hut doors are daubed: *Hutu. Tutsi.*
210   *You can go anywhere you like.*
You're quite safe. No harm will come to you.
                              No harm will come to you.
You are not that life, but another.
You are not the one must kill his mother.
You are not the death I must make
nor the death my life must take

beyond the painted door where my meaning lies
in the room where I hear no cries.

*

The people have gone to the church.
               Churches. Churches. Churches.
               Pastors. Priests. Bishops. Father. Father. Holy
Father.
Land is empty. Churches are full. Houses are broken. The forest is
cool
in the afternoon
of the happening
at Nyarubuye some time before,
where now the forest opens
its cupped hands
and lets the sun bleed its light
upon the carnage
that is happening, has been, is Being, is all that can ever be
that this witness ghost may see not see
that broke the bond between life and living
               in the story Leoncia Mukandayambaje tells
               of how she held her baby as a shield
               of how the baby's blood so covered her
               the killers thought they both were dead[4]
in that clearing
where the earth
cannot be seen
beneath the silence
               that is mine.
Where you see
               me.
Do not forget

220
230
240

me,
now you are all I have.
                    I watch you
wherever you go.
                    I will be with you.
                    You will remember
                              me.
                    The earth will eat
                              me.
                    The rain will wash
                              me.
                    I am the silence that you sense.
                    I am the life that is death.
                    I am living still.
                    I live with you.
                    Carry me away with you.
                    I am your eternity,
wherever there is eternity.
I am all that you see.
I am all I once was.
Do not look away.
                    I am not the maggots in my skull.
                    I am not my legs ripped wide for rape.
                    I am not the flies that feast my eyes.
                    I am not the arm torn from my shoulder.
                    I am not the stink of my rotting flesh.
                              I am all that you see.
                              I am all I once was.
Do not look away.
Tell me who I am
                                        I am
                                        I am
                                        I am

14

where my past lies
in your eyes.
You are the first
to come this way.
You are my witness.
Tell me who I am.
I am the dead
living now in you.
You will keep me living.
You will remember.
290 You are my witness.
I will live in you.
I am not the dead.
I will live in you.
You are my witness
            passing through the happening.
                  You pass among the dead who live
                        in memory
                              of the living
who made the dead.
300 The living and the dead. None living, none dead. All passing into
memory
as one body in time
as the voice of the one who watched the witness.

                  *

Pace the blood earth at Nyarubuye.
Pace the blood earth of Nyarubuye,
not as the living nor as the dead
but as witness
bearing the hollow
shaping the emptiness

310   grasping the void
        in those cupped hands of yours that wait, can wait, only for Time.
        For Time to be the Being.
        For Time to be forgetting.
        For Being to be forgotten in the passing.
        Being in Time. Time that will pass. Time that will pass from me.
        Time will not pass.
        Time cannot pass.
        There is no time
        on the blood earth
320   at Nyarubuye.
        There is no time.
        No past.
        No season. No month nor year.
        All is present.
        All is now
                        at Rwabusoro Bridge across the Akanyaru River.
        A battlefield is rotting animals
        and the Bibles of those who once passed through there.
        The invaders are winning now.
330   They are winning now,
        because all is lost.
        And some are winning now
        and some watch the fall of the *akazu*.
        And all is lost. All is lost
        among the eucalyptus
        by the swamp
        and the savannah
        that edge the church at Nyamata
        in this land
340   of burned shacks
        and bloody alters, bloody pulpits, bloody pews, bloody walls,
        bloody drapes clung by hands

wrenched into the mud heaped in the yard.
We took refuge in the swamp and hid under the papyrus,[5]
said Annonciata Umupfasoni,
sitting with outstretched legs
on a mattress beside the church,
gently rocking her daughter Harriett.
The Interahamwe caught us there.
350 *They cut me with a machete and spears.*
They came and spat in our eyes
and cut us
and hurled abuse.
They attacked us,
and then they left us five days' ago,
because the time for them to kill was over.

2: Prinsengracht 263

There is no past
360   behind the lock
locked
no entry
green door
facing
the cobbles
that clutch the come-and-go
of murmured recollections
in footsteps
that shift
370   forward
forward
forward a little
into the past that has not passed.
The step of steps on wooden steps
is the living,
who come to see
who is living among
the dead remembered in a smile captured

by the glass on which
380   reflections shuffle in a queue
aiming to again remember
remember one they never knew.

The canal drifts in ashen sun.
The canal drifts its own reflections
of a smile
of a smile.
Nothing is past.
There is no past behind the closed green door.
390   All is present
where footsteps clattered on the cobbles
where footsteps then came home from work
where footsteps carved last parables
of news of trains from Westerbork.[6]
 All stood present
  where at Albert-Ludwigs-Universität Freiburg[7]
die Wahrheit wird euch frei machen. Not toil
but *Truth Will Set You Free*
to watch Professor turn young soil[8]
400   and unearth the *Being* the youth would be
in that *Gleichschaltung*[9] Germany.
 All was present
  when young minds came to life again[10]
  and Professor hailed the thought-paths way[11]
and cast the *Sein und Zeit*[12] which lay
among the mind-games Führers play
  with all that is invisible
behind the
lock locked door
410   that opens onto cobblestones
where the ashen canal flows

with the *Being and Time* of *Wahrheit* bones.

What time?

What time had come when Professor wrote National Socialism
had long-awaited the moment to Be all it would become?[13]
What time had come when Professor pledged to nurture all that
was born of the fury that his Führer bore?[14]
What time had come when
among orchid lips and arnica
an orphan versed the ashen wind,
which blew dead gods from Todtnauberg
and stoked the flames in those who sinned?
What time had come that had been lost or perhaps had
never been?
What time had come when *there are no facts, only interpretations*?[15]
What time had come when bread fed men who slaved for meat
and neighbours vanished from your street?
What time had come when the cobbles scratched and voices cracked
and vengeance smirked on Prinsengracht?[16]
What time had come when Professor in his mountain hut
opened doors he could not shut?
Is there anyone left to tell?
Is there anyone who can tell
of the time
for which there may or may not be words,
of the time
no words could understand,
the time when life was screamed to silence
when all that could be said might not be said?

*

To be is to understand.
To know is to speak the words that seek you out.[17]
Much later, when the world told itself it was all over,
Professor and orphan walked among the arnica,
Heidegger the Nazi, Celan the orphan poet
tortured by the language through which he drank[18]
the black milk of daybreak.[19]
What is it to be
450   with Professor on his *Schwarzwald* slope
reflecting on the passing of the years
when there are no years and is no past?
            All is present
in the breath-turn[20] passed
between the orphaned word and the date it cast[21]
among the orchids.
            All is present
in words now torn out of silence[22]
drawn in turn among the mountains
460   at a missed encounter in the *Engadine*
when Celan lost the chance to speak
with one who'd lost the will to seek,[23]
and so spoke instead with one he met along the way,
his cousin Klein, who understood what it is to say:
the Jew, you know, what does he have that is really his own,
that is not borrowed, taken and not returned?[24]

My characters are all dead.
My characters are all living
470   in the diary of the smile that died
in the torment that is left behind
in letters scribed in ashen flame
the orphan to his mother wrote
but to which *no answer came.*[25]

My characters are all dead.
My characters are all living
in shadows stolen long ago[26]
by *volklich* tribes in martyr times,
480   whose conjured gods drank from the flow
of heathen blood and mythic rhymes
the *völkisch* gangs swear oaths they know.

Volkhaft. Volklich. Völkisch.
Populist. Communal. Folkloric.
What is it to *be*? What is it to be the *Being*, to be the *Being* in its
own time?
What is it to be of this *zeit und sein*?
Time and Being. It all made sense to you, Professor. Then it was the
490   time to be
all that men and women be
when fanatics arm their fantasy,
and their *volkhaft* spirit[27] and their *volklich* will[28]
bring blood to legends and dreams that fill
the darkness of Todtnauberg hill.[29]
                Professor, it all made sense,
the journey made towards the essence
you willed you would awaken.[30]
Awaken something lost
500   of Teuton myths
and *völkisch* deeds
the grand *Dasein*
your Führer breeds
from *Der Stürm* he wakes[31]
in pursuit of the Death
that is the Life he makes[32]
with all the world laid waste in pursuit

23

of the Death that is his sole truth.[33]
                    Truth.
510   Revenge.[34] For what the conscience told
        to men who craft their gods from dust,
        from forest trees or fields of gold,
        who cloak their dreams in ashen crust
        as dry as those false gods they trust.
        Revenge. On those who carved Mosaic laws,
        and saw the void from distant shores,
        whose mystery no Führer had yet crushed
        to become new Truth.[35]

                    *

                    Truth.
520   My characters are all dead.
        My characters are all living,
        the gangster with the *Freikorps* blade
        who knifed a teacher in cold blood
        and learned to love the price he paid,
        he is not mysterious.
        He is not extraordinary.
        He has a name.
        His name is Höss. His name is Rudolf.
        Rudolf Höss, whose prison years before his Führer came
530   were passed in searching who to blame
        for *aberrations*[36] and the right[37]
        the *völkisch* myths claimed as their rite.
        What is right and what is wrong[38]
        Höss asked when all was said and done.
        After all was said and done.
        All said and done
        supposed this one
        who winced on seeing the blood of others run,[39]

this prisoner in his cell
540   listening at the window
        to *human aberrations, depravities and passions*[40]
        spied in the abyss
        only hollow men can know.
        Yes, he is Höss,
        who pored his books on *racial research and heredity* –
        I was happiest when studying these subjects[41] –
        and what is right and what is wrong, was all that he would ask
        once all was said and done
        and his Führer's time had come
550   and there was so much work that must be done,
        like office clerks and working men
        with clipboards, so said his colleague Eichmann:
        Machinery. Grasping cogs within cogs.
        Like clockwork. Like clockwork.
        I saw the machinery of death. And I saw those who observed the process of the
        work. I saw them always repeating the work and they looked at the second-
        hands, which hurried; hurried like life to death. The greatest and cruellest
        dance of death of all time. That I saw, and I will describe it, as a warning.[42]
        As a warning.
560   Who does he see fit to warn? His is no warning. He is the warning.
        This is the way the world ends.[43]
        This is the way the world ends.
        This is the way the world ends.
        Can there be a warning? It is the machinery,
        the second-hands,
        which hurried;
        hurried
        like life to death
        as if they must,
570   as if unstoppable,
        once the machinery had started.
        Men. Women. Machinery. Where are you now, Professor? Still
        pondering the arnica?

Barbarism is only permissible among cultured people, you tell us.[44]
Are the Todtnauburg orchids blooming, this summer of 1939,
as you celebrate the end of all that made us what we are?[45]
Now you see your Führer. You are too late, Professor. Too late to
speak truth of this man in all his ecstasy.[46]
Yes. Yes. As ecstasy hollows to euphoria.[47]

580 Yes. Yes. The machinery is moving. The machinery is moving.
Tell us of the machinery, Professor. You love the machine,
Professor. The machine is a *necessity*. It is, you say, all that stops
your beloved Dictator losing his way.[48]
And what of the *völkisch* dream you now see sow the seeds of its
destruction?[49]
What of your Nazis now? It is too late. It is too late to say,
Professor, that you did not quite grasp[50] what these men would
become as they led the people onto the ashen plains of that
völkisch land.[51]

590 So you call it *imitation*.[52] And so the machinery of imitation turns.
The cogs bite tight. Who is there to imitate? Does this machine
imitate itself? Does it break? When does it break?
When does it break?
For sure,
only when all is said and done.
And when all was said and done, Eichmann later mused: *the Jew
was used – as so often in his history – even by the highest leadership of the
Reich, as a catalyst on whom all their failures, all the coming difficulties and
inconveniences, were to be blamed.*[53]

600

And so the imitations scream,
the *völkisch* dreams of *Being* bleed,
and men in machinations dream
that bad is good where Führer's lead
deep into the *weed and vines*[54]
while cattle trucks wait on railway lines.

3: Tawantinsuyu

Parched space.
610   Rock.
Dry timelessness.[55]
Raw.
Vast.
Gouged black cold white heat.
Ice. Burn. Ice. Burn.
Above. Between. Below.
Sensed.
Time and timeless. Black. Cold. White. Heat.
Sensed.
620   Named and nameless. Told. Spoken. Said.
Far. Near.
Eye. Hand.
Makers.
Made.
Seen.
Distance.
Above.
Between.
Below.
630   I. You. We.
Move.
In shadow. In light. In darkness. Light. Dark.

The parched spaces.
Move.
Through. Past. Beyond. Above. Above.
We move through the landscape; it does not move through us.[56]
Move through the mouth of the land.
Move up. Light in darkness. Eyes watch from light that is darkness.
Above. Between. Below.

640
Here is nowhere. We are nowhere. We are here. We are
somewhere.
Parched space.

Then the water came.

Deep in the darkness of *Nun* an egg cracked.

Land rose from that water, bearing *Atum*, golden as the sun.[57]

650
Then the water came.
Deep in the darkness of Titicaca, a body stirred.
From the water Inti's children rose, dressed as gods in royal
clothes.[58]
The water.
The water. Snake.
The water. Curling red silver.
The water. What will the thunder voice bring?
The water, from where the eight brothers and sisters
were saved when the flood tide drained.[59]

660
Manco Capac
Ayar Cache
Ayar Uchu
Ayamanco
Mama Huaco
Mama Ocllo

Mama Ragua
Mama Cura.

We are eight who survived the flood. We are the Children of Inti-
Sun.[60]

670 We have our myths.
Many.
Not all the same.
Many myths, same flood.

*

*They say that a month before the flood came, the sheep displayed much sadness,
eating no food in the day-time, and watching the stars at night. At last the
shepherd, who had charge of them, asked what ailed them, and they said that
the conjunction of stars showed that the world would be destroyed by water.
When he heard this, the shepherd consulted with his six children, and they
agreed to collect all the food they could, and to go to the top of the very high*

680 *mountain, called Ancasmarca. They say that as the waters rose, the mountain
grew higher, so that it was never covered by the flood, and when the waters
subsided, the mountain also grew smaller.[61]*

The peak of Ancasmarca rose above the water.
The peak of Ancasmarca saved the shepherd and his children.
    The wolves of Parnassus rose above the water.
    The howling of the wolves guided the Lykoreians to Parnassus.[62]
Deucalion and Pyrrha landed on Parnassus,
everywhere else being drowned by the waters.[63]

690   On the mountain of Nimush the boat ran aground.
        Mount Nimush held the boat fast, allowed it no motion,
        so Uta-napishti told Gilgamesh as he sought
immortality.[64]
Mountains as saviours.[65]
Rock as Maker.

Maker as Meaning.
Meaning as Rock.[66]
Rock. The life of Tawantinsuyu.
Rock shaped by the Children of the Sun.
700   Rock torn from the bones of Antisuyu.
Rock nourished where wild waters run.
We move through the landscape; it does not move through us.
And plunder the land and stars
for meaning.
For Meaning,
in the knot of the *quipu* code
the *quipucamayoc* show
had Meaning when the *camay*[67] essence was made to flow
to *camascas* rock and *camascas* stars[68]
710   to untouched peaks and clutched *huacas*
the will the *camayoc* brought to Being.
            Being.
            Time and Being
            Brought into Being.
            Made to Be
a universe that could only Be
that could not Be without the Meaning the *camay* gave
the clay
from which Creator Viracocha
720   shaped the nations
and dressed their peoples with the clothes of peoples
and gave life and soul to each one
and ordered that they rise from the subterranean space
and become the peoples of the earth[69]
in the empty silent place
among the *huacas*
that bind the bonding *ceque* lines
to the light and dark and season signs

31

the forest clouds will shadow from the heights of
730   Antisuyu.
                Antis.
                    Andes
the *runa simi*[70] tongue then named
once the waters had been tamed
and the universe the *Being* dreamed
came to be all *Being* seemed
        in rocks and rivers and mountain skies,
        where into thunder the *kuntur* flies
        between the stars of Qoyllur
740   upon the starlit Mayu Way,
        where the forest cloud now blows
across a universe the season grows,
when Illapa's thunder-water flows
through rock carved by the canal *yarqa*[71]
above the roar of Vilcanota
from the mountain lake of Cularcocha
to feed the mind of Pachacutec,
the stars now cast from high Apu
into shadow here at Machu Picchu.
750

                *

A thousand steps above the Lucre *huaca*,
the humming *colibrí* hover in suspended crucifixion,
like blazing eyes among the orchid tongues of the *wiñay huayna*,
fragile petals,
jewels among the crag of peaks
and the Cordillera shard,
which tears the staggering sky that speaks
760   in the seasons of the sundial yard.

Aticsi-Viracocha caylla-Viracocha tocapo ac nupo viracochan, Thou art without equal unto the ends of the earth. Thou who givest life and strength to mankind, saying, let this be a man and let this be a woman. And as thou sayest, so thou givest life, and vouchsafest that men shall live in health and peace, and free from danger – Thou who dwellest in the heights of heaven, in the thunder, and in the storm clouds, hear us, and grant us eternal life. Have us in thy keeping, and receive this our offering, as it shall please thee, O Creator.[72]

770

Rock.
Water.
Light.
Dark.
Uku Pacha beneath the world, where serpent river Vilcanota coiled.
Kay Pacha upon the land, the *tunkuy* where the puma prowled.
Hanan Pacha. There. Far above. The place beyond the highest peaks,
where *kuntur* soars and Illapa speaks
780   where condor glides and thunder guides
the water feeding mountainsides
crafted by the mason's hand
from andesite to farmer's land.
      Above. Below. Between.
      What is known is what is seen
and what is dreamed is what is mapped
between solstice and the thunder cracked
  when equinox is time to sow
and Inti-Sun melts mountain snow.
790   It is warm where the temple stones
          bear the weight of *kuntur* bones.
It is soft, the wind that blows through Machu Picchu.
It is silent in the Temple of the Sun.

All noise is imagined. The serpent Vilcanota flows so far below, it
is silent.

Once, the *qollqa* brimmed the final harvest,
the farmers put away their hoes,
the condor flew across the range
and Inti shone his final glows
into his dear Quilla's eyes.
      Inti
            Quilla
      Inti
            Quilla,
the light and the dark
the husband and wife
the day the night
the sun the moon
            Inti
            Quilla.
Tunkuy where all opposites meet
where two as one make one,
silver as gold
gold as silver
sun moon
moon sun
the heat the cold
the day the night.
All one
among the rain and rock
        and you are mine
        and I am yours
        and we are one
where all is known and all unknown
and all is mapped and all is strange

800

810

820

and all is lost that once was known
when the dead returned to stone
      along the royal *capac nan*[73] roads of Tawantinsuyu,[74]
830   an empire bound to earth and star
      by sacred gold and sculped ashlar
that is the living rock of Sacsahuamán,
what to one God's pirate was a castle
but to believers was the temple Sun[75]
scaled to Inca's model mountains
on the heights above Cuzco's fountains.
      There was no castle.
The Inca won enemies over to their rule by gifts and promises.[76]
      There was no castle.
840 *It was by artfulness and gentle words rather than by force that the Inca
achieved his conquest.*[77]
      There was no castle.
*The Inca are peaceable and have certain good habits which make life easy for
them.*[78]
      There was no castle.
The Inca understood that there was more to man than the mortal body.[79]
      There was no castle.
*When there was no war, the supplies of food were divided up among the poor
and the widows.*[80]
850   There was no castle.
*They built irrigation ditches. As the rivers never dry, the Inca conduct water
where they will.*[81]
      And the walls told stories
      of their long journeys
      from the quarries of
Waqoto, Rumiqolqa Yucay and Muina.
      Tired rocks. Bleeding rocks[82]
      dragged from the places of their birthing
      to the places where the Inca building

860	formed the stones to mimic mountains
	shaping rock to scaled massif
	a miniature world in model form
	a universe in Inca's palm
	at Huacaypata in Cuzco square
	where the *ceque* and *capac nan* all met
	at the *usnu* of Tawantinsuyu,[83]
	where the sun line rays and Royal Roads
	mapped land and prayer, work and water,
	to the golden hall of Qorikancha
870	where the Punchao image of Inti's gold
	was Meaning never to be bought or sold

and *it should be known that although in one province they eat human flesh and make human blood sacrifices, there are many others who abhor this sin. And if in others they indulge in the sin against nature, in many they hold it to be a foul thing, and never commit, and on the contrary, loathe it. Therefore, it would be unjust to condemn them all. And even these evils which they committed have the excuse that they lacked the light of our Holy Faith, and for that reason they were unaware of the wrong they were doing, like many other nations, especially the Gentiles in olden times, who, like these Inca, lacking the light of faith, made as many sacrifices as they did, and more.*[84]

	But so it was that pirate lords,
	armour-clad with bandit swords
	rode Royal Roads as *conquistadores*.
	And so it was, the chronicler told,
	of how they filled their mouths with Inti's gold,
	and wove Punchao's blood in gaudy chains
	and savaged the land of holy rains
890	from a time and date the sundial drew
	24 September 1532.

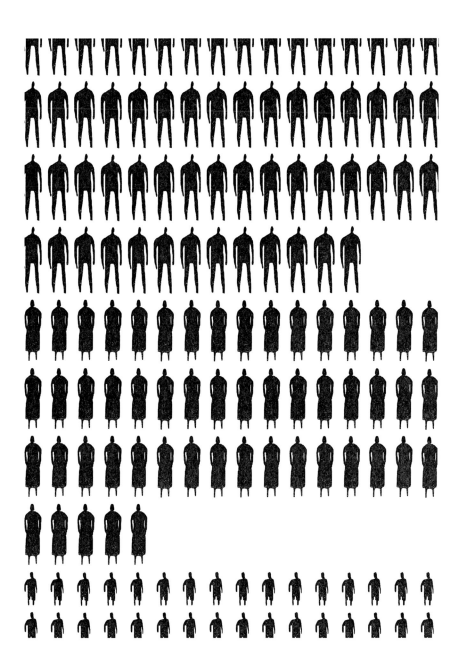

37

4: Am Großen Wannsee 56–58

The meeting was closed
with the request of the Chief of the Security Police and the SD
to the participants
that they afford him
900   *appropriate support*
during the carrying out
of the tasks
involved in
the solution[85]
that is the beginning
recorded in the Minutes,
that is the beginning without the end
that began.

910   *Perhaps. Perhaps we can say*
that every poem is marked by
its own '20th of January'?[86]
So he told his audience in Darmstadt.
They had given him a prize, Paul Celan.
It was October 1960
and he had received the Georg Buchner Prize.
Ladies and Gentlemen, he told them:
The poem speaks.

It is mindful of its dates,
920   *But it speaks.*
True, it speaks only on its own,
its very own behalf.
It knows its dates. It knows when it started.
It knows when it began
its short, endless life.
That beginning without an end.
Not October. But January.
The 20th of January.
The 20th of January.
930   *It is mindful of its dates.*
The poem is lonely. It is lonely and en route.
Its author stays with it,[87]
both the poem
and the man borne of that day
born that day
born
into the winter of the moment
fringed by the rowing club jetties that have closed for the season.

940   *I can no longer say if the phrase*
'final solution of the Jewish question'
was coined by me or if it originated from Müller.[88]
To coin
a phrase.
Thank you, Adolf Eichmann, for your phrase,
efficiently recorded
in the Minutes you took
of the Meeting
that
950   day
that 20th of January

the 20th of January 1942.
That day
der Endlösung der Judenfrage
posed a riddle for the fifteen men
who paced parquet floors warmed from the grate
in winter light etched by wood-panelled walls.
Cherub babes playing at guarding the gate
watched where the portico led to the halls

960   where it was decided that death would become life
where death was no longer entwined *in epic unity with a full life.*[89]
Where it was decided that death would be life itself.
It was decided,
and State Secretary Doctor Bühler told the meeting
that the General Government would welcome it
if the final solution
of this problem
could be begun in the General Government.[90]
It was decided.

970   It was not a question
being asked by those *small, cheap, miserable minds without any character*
to whom only the tinsel of their high rank or the executive capacity of their
position, in the days of their glory, lent the necessary image and posture[91]
Eichmann would reminisce,
his
terrifyingly normal[92]
truth
of words once spoken
seeming proof

980   that all was true for being said
first by the leaders then by the led
with their *camouflage words:*
special treatment
migration to the east

transfer to the east for work deployment
evacuation to the east
final solution of the Jewish question.
All could mean
that those identified
990   *as such*
could be killed,[93]
as impatient hands tap the mantelpiece,
the cherub's harp silent as the bow
the marble player strummed to summer's lease
turned ashen-faced beyond the window,
where geese skimmed the Wannsee like before
beyond the chestnut and the lawn
that slips so gently to the lakeside shore
where January the 20th had been born,
1000   and where all is present
        in a footstep stride
up the elegant sweep of the spiral stair
into the privacy of the rooms up there,
where a leathered hand taps a mantelshelf
and men ask after the children's health.
Do send my regards to Frau Heydrich, do
send my greetings to your children too.
With so much valuable work to be done
they will miss you, Eichmann, till we have won.

          *

1010   And all is present
        in the shift of the trees
        that blow like Nature
        in a gentle breeze.
And all is present,

as Professor mutters his mild lament
that all that has happened is not what he meant,
as the *volklich* will he dreamed shone bright[94]
became skin, hair, ash, flame
from the chimney Mrs Schächter foresaw[95]

1020   through the window grate of the cattle truck from Sighet
Marmaţiei
many days before
a destination
had been reached.
A destination
had been reached
Professor dreamed would bring the light[96]
his German kin could cast on night[97]
alone and so become the story.

1030   *Volklich.* Folkloric.
A story to tell the grandchildren.
And do send my regards to Frau Heydrich.
Do send my greetings to your children too.
They will have such stories to tell.
They will have such stories.
The stories
witnessed by one
who knows
he cannot escape

1040   the moral demand
to confront
those who
would enjoy their moment
of knowing
their crimes had been forgotten.[98]
The forgetting of the dead
is to kill them a second time,[99]

these *pieces*[100] in the cattle truck,
who had been bussed from Fossoli
1050   to the station at Carpi.
The *pieces* who knew nothing of infinity.
Forty-one *pieces* who did not see their homes again.[101]
Four from forty-five, who would see their homes again.
None can know infinity.
There is infinity.
It is the emptiness of pine forests
It is a quiet country station
It is the dark silent plateau
alive to nothing but the rhythm of the wheels
1060   moving
as the administration had arranged
      moving
through emptiness life and death deranged
within emptiness. A world hollowed.
        Wordless life haunts darkness.
Life haunts.
      Life is the haunted darkness.
          Life is darkness
when in an official apparatus
1070   *nobody can*
do and permit
what he wants,
but everybody acts
according to
orders[102]
issued from darkness into darkness
by human hand to human hand
mind to mind
voice to voice
1080   place to place.

43

Mind. Voice. Place.
The truths that are not some other life.
Truths that are among us. Now. Today, just one moment past
on the parting of a train
whose destination sign remains
a murmur on the ashen breath
of those who will remember
and those who never saw
what Vistula's current bore

1090   as silt to nourish Kraków's shore,
carried just one moment past
from Westerbork and Košice
from Drancy into *völkisch* lore
on clipboard lists in briefcase files
by men on whom the deaths-head smiles
from birth that spawns first envy then revenge.

Our strength in the executive lay not in creative action,
but in our complete supervision.
1100   *We did not need at all to be creative*
because every phase of a procedure
was already considered
and thought through
by other minds [103]
Eichmann logistician wrote.
I only took care of the transports
and the legal support
in individual countries
under our influence
1110   *so that they would deliver their Jews to us.*
Everything else I did not wish to see,
and did not wish to have anything to do with.
In the case of the transportations,

the only consolation
was that I did not even know
who would die and who not die.[104]

Consoled.
To know.
1120   Not to know.
All were to die. Immediately or later. All were to die. It said so in
the Minutes of that 20th of January. That day to which he alone
gave birth
by writing it into existence.
He did not know *who would die and who not die.*
There was no *who.*
The *pieces* were not *who.*
The *pieces* were *pieces.*
The *pieces* were *transports.*
1130   There was no *who.*
Their names were not the names of people.
They were *pieces* in a puzzle, and *if any of the deportees were killed, who*
they were or how many I did not know, for this did not fall within my sphere of
duties[105]
detailed in the orders
issued from darkness into darkness
by human hand to human hand
mind to mind
voice to voice
1140   place to place.
Mind. Voice. Place.
The truths that are not some other life.
Truths that are among us. Now. Today,
    aboard the 09.11 train R34404 for Oświęcim
    that will be leaving in one hour and eleven minutes
on a journey through infinity

to what lies beyond
mind voice place
made on that day

1150   the 20th of January was born
and then became
all that Mrs Schächter had imagined
when she warned the people in the cattle truck,
warned of fire, warned of flames,
but was silenced
till she again told what she imagined
to the people in the truck
and warned of fire and warned of flames,
but was silenced till she again told the people in the truck

1160   of the fire and of the flames
which struck them all to silence
when they finally saw what she had warned them of
rising into the night sky.[106]

And today the 09.11 train R34404 for Oświęcim.
Will be leaving in an hour.
Across the gentle roll of hills
to where the stream of Soła spills
into Vistula and the land beyond
infinity, drifting fine as sand

1170   into the flow
that passed below
the bridge at Monowice.

And so the Oświęcim train departs
to where today each journey starts
with a whistle from the commuter train
to one who never was his brother's Cain[107]
among the saved who, once returned,
could not put words to what they'd learned.[108]

5: Inyenzi

Land clings to its beginnings,
1180   myth in memory
until memory became *mythico-history*[109]
    of a time before these days, when *people kill for ten francs,*[110]
    of a time before the homeland,
      the *heimat*[111] of the *akazu,* utopia's *völkisch* dream-come-true,
was buried beneath the laterite.

The ice sweat face has its plan in mind.
    They have worked the land, those fists.
    They have worked the land, those eyes.
1190   They have the plan in mind.

It is the 8th of January 1994.
This is the northern edge of Kigali, and
today's beginning
is a road junction
wreaking jagged with machetes
in the hands of the sons and daughters
of those who in '59
broke up a myth of power
1200   *being held by the privileged family and group.*[112]
        Three decades have past.

Today, these children are men and women
whose beginning
is fear
of themselves
of the other,
of their own people
and its clans,
of what is known and seen and heard
1210 of what is told and blamed and learned
from the clansmen of the *akazu*, who speak
of the pure and the impure,
of who from the north of who from the south
of who the for and who the against
in *the history of the Hutu and Tutsi,*
story of Cain and Abel,
brothers who no longer understand each other
because of mere nothings[113]
that haunt the hollow night
1220 with fear of being outcast from the pure clan
of Kanzinga and her brothers
She offered advice on how to neutralise opposition among women[114]
of Bagasora and his officers
The chiefs were contacted, to see who was opposed to the President[115]
of Kajuga and his squad
I'm shocked. For me it's the RPF who have created the problems...the violence[116]
of Habyarimana and his loyalists
The Prefet said burn down the houses of people who are not supporters of the President[117]
of Mugenzi and his faction
1230 *People are saying: be careful, because the Tutsis may come with their guns.*[118]

And the myths perhaps are true.
The myths perhaps are false.
There may be no myth

of the Shem-Hamitic *wahuma*
travelling south from Abyssinia,
the guesswork of John Hanning Speke – grand imperial
adventurer.
There may be no reason to turn the thousand hills to

1240 graveyards[119]

> *in these kingdoms*
> *where the government*
> *is in the hands*
> *of foreigners*
> *of which a marked characteristic is*
> *a bridged*
> *instead of a bridgeless*
> *nose.*[120]

And it happened *for reasons that cannot be traced.*[121]

1250 It may have happened *because of mere nothings.*
Perhaps it happened without language,
   for *Being is language, and as such it is understandable.*[122]
What happened may have happened
because Being is not language, Minister Mugenzi hints,
telling me how
there's a Tutsi consciousness
which stops them from living with other Rwandese
in harmony
they look to the past with regrets – their past power

1260 *they try to cultivate*
their ethnic group pride
this is why
all along
through the centuries
they have refused to mix with the Hutus
otherwise how do you explain the fact
that you still manage to spot them

they have consciously refused to integrate
the Hutus have a greater readiness
1270 *to integrate*
and forget
as long as the Tutsis
don't behave
in a revolting manner[123]
he ruminates,
forming a half-smile that will Be the Being
when killing the *inyenzi* cockroach starts,
when killing becomes the Being
and nothing is forgotten
1280 that was ever known
and the language is the killing
and the killing is the Meaning
as the men rage waiting
for the *inkotanyi* warriors,
here,
at the road junction jagged with machetes.

The ice sweat face has its plan in mind.
They have worked the land, those fists.
1290 They have worked the land, those eyes.
They have the plan in mind

for reasons that cannot be traced
nor known
nor unknown, but for sure
says Lieutenant Wenceslas of the *Gendarmerie Nationale*, pointing at
me,
usually the Tutsis look just like you
they are tall
1300 *and have long, straight noses*

51

but I don't know any of them
I don't know any Tutsis
none of them have ever been my friends
not one
never[124]
after a thousand years have passed
and the time has come to choose
who will be the past and who the future
the choice soon in the hands of neither,
1310   but of those who work the land,
the wreaking hands of raging men
whose silhouettes haunt the Great Lakes hills
with the *ideology of extermination,*[125]
the lawyer in his Kigali *cabinet*
confiding with quiet resignation
that *the only way to change things*
is if politics is based on the majority of ideas[126]
that the clans and factions forge as creed
the farmers then can plant as seed
1320   across the hills where children feed
to another rhythm. Take a Primus in the *cabaret*
with neighbours kneeling there to pray
with you in the hilltop chapel. It is there again,
the fever, *a madness that went on all by itself*[127]
just like '59 and '73
when the leaders conjured war by stealth
and you burned your neighbour before he could flee
to where the *inkotanyi* passed the years
in patient exile the *akazu* fears
1330   will end with guns and not with spears
when the *inyenzi* come to claim what's theirs
        among the rolling oceans of the hills.

Let us reason to hate, and imagination stirs.
Let us reason our hate.
We have a reason to hate.
Let us hate.
Let us rage our hate.
We shall hate.
1340   I will hate.
Will you hate with me?
Hate me. I will hate you too.
We shall hate
      together.
      It will bind us
      when the *inyenzi* come
from the time king-*mwami* ruled the valleys
where some kept cattle and others tilled land,
and one was *hutu* the other *tutsi*
1350   whose courtly power was the king enthroned[128]
      among the ocean *milles collines*,
where Prussian knights then Belgian priests
          turned foetal lands to mission feasts
and imperial powers bought and sold the king
who created the myth he was key to everything
and that without the king there would be no rain[129]
Minister Mugenzi opined,
as he dwelt upon history's pain, so *the Tutsis*
like the Jews have remained always
1360   *and waited for the day of revenge.*
And now the situation is tense
because the Tutsis are too anxious to take power,
and the Hutus aren't prepared to accept that.[130]
And so let us hate
and rage our hate
upon the *mwami* kin and acolytes

53

who ruled as servants of the whip-hand whites
                    who knelt in cassocks at their Sunday prayers
                    in a house whose God was not yours but theirs
1370   who plumped on gifts the courtiers preyed
              and closed the gates on those who strayed
                    back in the time of princelings,
                    when the *hutu* bought his *tutsi* name
                    and the migrant myth of invader kings
                    had yet to be what it became
              when empires made mythic tribes of their own great game,[131]
              and what once was water turned to flame
              as holy fathers clawed power from earth
              and gambled *mwami* was not worth
1380   saving for his royal birth
              when the time came to hand the church-door key
              to the righteous ones who must be free
              to forgive the priests for their duplicity.
              And so let us wait
              until the day when what was yours is mine
              that day in 1959
              when feudal *mwami* and his acolytes
              lost favour with God and the whip-hand whites,
              and fled the land of the *milles collines*
1390   and the forests turned to red from green
              as we raged the hate we loved to hate
              and lived the deaths our times create
                    to be the meaning
              that is all our lives must be
              when the imagination stirs
              and different forces try to use the situation and exploit the ethnic
              background[132]
              from the time before,
              when the *mwami* ruled

54

1400   and the royal lore
       was all the truth the people saw
             as revolution the *akazu* guard
             by naming your tribe on your ID card.

       There was a situation of imbalance during the feudal system
       during which the Hutu were being exploited,
       though this was also happening
       to some of the lower-class Tutsis[133]
             the *inyenzi* chief Kagame tells
1410   at his Mulindi base among the hills,
       where this listener hears this refugee
       shame the failed history
       that is the whip-hand's legacy, for
       when they left they never addressed the question of harmony,
       and in fact they strengthened the ethnic tension[134]
       that might become
       might not become
       that might be memory
       and might be past
1420   but which became
       the universe in which the *akazu* build
       the place where they have *inyenzi* killed
             to make their history real, as
       events have made people aware of ethnicity,
       but the basic question is one of human rights and governance.
       You find a lot of exaggeration of ethnicity,
       Kagame tells me
       as that day falls to evening
       and I leave him there
1430   and wonder if we will meet again,
       as the United Nations takes me back
       to where the highway meets the track

and we reach the checkpoint boundary
that speaks not of time nor history
but darkness, which has no time nor word,
just the sound that once heard
becomes a wordless destiny
                    and the question is no longer asked:
where do you come from
1440   what is your place
what is the place you call your home.
But it was never asked again
of women alone with lonely men
there at the junction that is jagged with machetes.

          The ice sweat face has its plan in mind.
                    They have worked the land, those fists.
                    They have worked the land, those eyes.
          They have the plan in mind.

6: Chapaghjur

1450

Look, The Euphrates is Flowing with Blood.[135]
Fırat suyu kan akıyor baksana.
Sarikamiş is a forest area.
The army was stationed in the middle of the forest.
On waking in the morning we realized
that the entire army
had been swallowed by the snow.
We could see nothing – not our frozen tents nor the forest.
We dug our way out through holes

1460   *and found we were covered with lice.*[136]

Look, The Euphrates is Flowing with Blood
and Saci Efendi,
official with the Imperial Office of Foreign Affairs,
flees Sarıkamış to drown in the snows of Kars.
Eve dönüş. The Long Way Home.[137]
It is the track whose stones are frozen men.
It is the chestnut mare whose breath is ice.
It is the peak of Allahuekber Mountain
Whose story ends among the lice.

1470   Home.
                    Byzantium.
                            Turania.

Sarıkamış. Sarıkamış.

58

17 January 1915. Eastern Anatolia.

There are majestic ranges called the Allahuekbar Mountains.
They too were covered with snow.
We fled – the Russians hot on our heels.
Our army reached the mountains
and came face to face with the Russians – bayonet to bayonet.

1480   *There was no one left in our battalion.*[138]

       Defeat.
       Blame.
       Hunt for traitors.
       Hunt the traitors.

         17 January 1915. Eastern Anatolia.
         Blame.
            Hunt for traitors.
                Hunt the traitors.

Anyone who did not see the Battle of Sarıkamış has seen nothing of the
1490   *world.*[139]

         17 January 1915. Eastern Anatolia.

If you have not seen all this, it's because you have not seen anything at all,[140]

         and all it was
         that had not been seen
         could then become
         what had not been
         and all that had
         not been known
         could become
1500   what would be known.

            But now, as Yaşar Kemal writes
                to tell the truth of men,
            the Young Turk Talaat Paşa
                takes his place again

among folklore fears and vengeful rites
the tribes and *çetis* have in their sights

from Sarikamiş and the Caucasus front to the Dersim and the desert.
Hunt for traitors.
Hunt the traitors.

1510   among Ottoman ranks whose imperial dead
were left to freeze by those who fled,
and who this day live by the guile
of careers built upon denial
    that hate needs its story,
    that hate shapes its world,
    while on the open market
    the truth is priced in gold
that today gilds the words of courtiers
    who talked of revolt when there was none

1520   and rebel arsenals where there were none
and revolution when there was none
and claim that Armenian rebels were preparing for war[141]
when no rebel force nor guns were numbered[142]
    while Sarikamiş burned its frozen flame,
    a mountainside where an empire died.
    But the dead never spoke of who to blame,
    and could never silence those who cried
about the traitors who were not,
and the loyal ones who fought –

1530   those Armenian sons who rot
for the Sultanate's Sublime Porte[143]
as it shattered into the pieces of its peoples:
    Muslim
    Christian
    Turk
    Armenian
    Slav
    Arab
    Circassian

1540   Persian
                   Kurd
                   Egyptian
                          Berlin
                               Paris
                                     London
            and Petrograd fought the Caucasian storms
            as Talaat fired young Ottoman hearts,
            that fell to the freeze in martyr's tombs
            at Sarikamiş as his genocide starts.
1550

                        *

The Armenian Genocide
was both the result
of increasingly radical attitudes
of Turkish national imperialists,
and was triggered by the events of 1914-1915:
the imposition of the European reform plan;
the breakdown of CUP-Armenian relations
1560   *when the Dashnaks refused to instigate rebellion among Caucasian Armenians;*
        the colossal loss at Sarıkamış;
        and the rapid reconstruction of the Armenians as an imminent danger.[144]

                   Sarıkamış.

Death of men.
            Death of nation.
                   Death of a people.
                          Death of truth
1570   across a ravaged land,
            where weak men took the upper hand
            when hate was loosed to make its stand

as truth the savage eats to make the hollow times seem grand.
                    All was made, *reconstructed*
into the life of war-time
into the time of war-life
into a time when the threatened storm *which had been brewing for a*
long time[145]
turned savage hope to savage crime
turned savage dream to savage time
turned man to dog, turned life to lime
across the hollow land where the only truth was hate, the only
dream was death,
where the future was revenge for Byzantium's last breath
                    no god playing its part, as
                    I can personally testify
                    that Talaat Pasha
                    cared nothing for Mohammedanism
                    for, like most of the leaders of his party,
                    he scoffed at all religions[146]
while a border lay beneath the snows of Karş
and frightened men mapped empire dreams[147]
then conjured from the moon and stars
a people drowned in their own screams,
                    so Aurora learned
                    from Mrs Abouhayatian,
                    who told of how her husband in Van
                    went to remonstrate with the *Vali* Governor Djevdet Bey
                    that he should protect the Armenians,
                    and the *Vali* uttered words famous till today:
                    Ishim yok. Keifim tchok.
                    I have no work to do. I have much fun.[148]
                    Ishim yok
                    Keifim tchok
                    said the famous *Horse-shoer of Basshkale,*[149]

1580
1590
1600

62

so-called *for this connoisseur in torture*
had invented what was perhaps
the masterpiece of all —
that of nailing horseshoes
1610 *to the feet*
of his Armenian victims.[150]
                    Hunt the traitors
as *there is little question*
that Djevdet Bey
came to Van
with definite instructions
to exterminate all Armenians in the Province,[151]
            to hunt the traitors,
            hunt them down.
1620   *Yar, Vur, Oldur.*
                    20 April 1915, Van:
Djevdet Bey
orders 4,000 Armenian men
to present themselves
to fight for the empire
that is torturing them.
Bey's order is ignored,
so he accuses the Armenians of
revolution.
1630   20 April 1915, Van:
soldiers seize several Armenian women in the city.
The men who try to rescue them are shot dead.
Fighting erupts.
The city is burning.
The Bey has fabricated the
revolution
that is the excuse he needs
            for hate needs its story.

63

Hate shapes its world.
1640   There, see it among the eucalyptus.
                       It is smoke now,
where Djevdet Bey
orders the arrest of Mr Ishkhan and Deputy Vramiam,[152] though
                       the government should have known
                       that through these actions
                       they had finally caused the infuriation
                       which had been brewing for a long time,[153]
the Ottomans' German ally
Scheubner-Richter
1650   told his Ambassador Wangenheim,
who relayed to Reichskanzler Bethmann Hollweg
that the Armenians
have given up their ideas
of a revolution.[154]
                       But in defeat
                       lay the blame
                       and hunt for traitors,
even when in Marash *these measures by the Central Government*
                       are based on a basic conception
1660   *that is false; it considers the entire Armenian population*
                       to be suspicious or even hostile[155]
even when *the insurrection in Diyarbekir,*
                       is therefore probably a result
                       of the mistreatment of the Armenians[156]
even when in Zeitoun *there is*
                       now not a case of a planned, general riot;
                       above all, they do not have the weapons for such an act.[157]
                       But hate needs its story
                       and hate shapes its world,
1670   there, among the eucalyptus,
                       when decisions made

                    need their reason
                    and plans then laid
                    for the killing season
          play on the minds of the murderer
          while spicing the words of those who seem
                    intent upon the make believe
                    that *if one asserts,*
                    as many modern Armenian voices do,
1680   *that the Armenians were simply defending themselves,*
                    how can one explain
                    that it was the Armenians
                    who made the first attack?[158]
          a claim today's defender feels no need
          to substantiate with facts. So we read
          hollow riddles, no purpose served
          but the strange comfort
          that the dead of Van got what they deserved
                    even while Berlin told its ally truths
1690   defenders now insist they must defy
          while from Erzurum the Young Turks' ally Scheubner-Richter wrote
                    that *weapons had been assembled for some time now —*
                    in the earlier stages for the purpose of self-defence only
                    against an eventual massacre,
                    but later also for the purpose of an armed uprising.
                    That ongoing mistakes have been committed by the Turks
                    in the handling of the Armenian question
                    is known only too well by Your Excellency.[159]

                              *

          No secret there,
1700   only truth, for a people threatened with extinction.
          No secret there,

that *the deportation orders*
can no longer be justified by military considerations;
rather, it is a matter of destroying the Armenians,
as Talaat Bey told me several weeks ago,[160] Germany's
Consul Mordtmann wrote
while Wangenheim wrote to Bethmann Hollweg
that *this situation*
and the way in which the relocation is being carried out
shows that the government is indeed pursuing its purpose
of eradicating the Armenian race from the Turkish Empire.[161]
No revolt
nor *revolution,*
the German ally making no secret that
Isolated incidents,
such as armed resistance in the case of requisitions in faraway vill
the killing of Turks who wanted Armenian girls and women han
over to them,
or the cutting and sabotaging of telegraph and telephone lines,
and espionage
are not unusual phenomena
during a war
in border areas
containing mixed populations.[162]
but still the denialist insists that
rebellion in Van began before the beginning of the war[163]
though where and when remains a mystery to many.
But still the denialist insists that
the Van revolt
was the main factor
that convinced the Ottoman government
to take steps
to stop Armenians from acting elsewhere,
as they had in Van,

by relocating Armenians.[164]

And still the denialist insists

Revenge was unquestionably a motive in Muslim attacks on Armenians[165]

And still the denialist insists

The only way one can speak of a genocide of Armenians in World War One
is by conveniently not mentioning the Armenian rebellion
and not counting the Muslim dead[166]

And still the denialist insists

Both the forces of the Armenian Republic
and the most important 'other authority' of the Armenians,
the Dashnak Party,
were guilty of the mass slaughter of Muslims[167]

And still the denialist insists

No one has ever found evidence of any Ottoman attempt to kill all the Armenians.[168]

And still the denialist insists

It was not genocide, it was war.[169]

*

But what is to be gained from this denial?

What is to be gained from denial

when the guilt of the guilty has been revealed by their accomplices:

I was in contact with Talaat Bey and personally received the annihilation order,
Abdul'ahad Nuri Bey
told Ihsan Bey,
Head of the Special Bureau of the Interior Ministry.[170]
These atrocities,
committed according to a clear programme
and with absolute intent,
were carried out at the orders and supervision of,
first, members of the Union and Progress Central Committee,

and, second,

by leading members of the government,[171]

1770   the Commander of the Ottoman Third
Army

Vehip Paşa would later say,

confirming all that Talaat Paşa wrote

in cipher cables which leave no doubt

that *it had previously been communicated*

that the government,

by order of the Cemiyet committee,

had decided

to completely annihilate

1780   *all Armenians living in Turkey*[172]

while

Those who oppose

this command and decision

cannot remain part of the official structure of the state,[173]

where neighbour must turn against neighbour

by feeding the savage that prowls within

by freeing the *çetis* from prison cells

to slaughter the pure and orgy with sin

while on a piece of paper

1790   all that happened

is explained

in answer to

The Question, to which

the Vali replied very coldly

that there was no possibility of changing the order in any

way,

as it had been sent in just that form

from Constantinople[174]

and so was conceived

1800   and planned

and ordered
and issued
as an organised way
to address

The Question

the Ottoman's mercenary Nogales heard not asked but told in Van,
                    where the Vali *astounded me by replying*
1810   *that he was doing nothing more than carry out*
                    an unequivocal order
                    emanating from the Governor-General of the province
                    to exterminate all Armenian males of twelve years of age
                    and over[175]
        then to address

The Question

he heard answered in Diyarbekir in a telegram of three words:
1820   *Yar, Vur, Oldur.*
                    Burn, demolish, kill.[176]
                    The Question that is no question.
That Question
                    esâslı bir suretde hal ve fasli ile külliyen izâlesi.
That Question that will be
                    brought to an end in a comprehensive and absolute
                    way.[177]
That Question
                    die Frage
1830 Germany's Consul Mordtmann discussed with Talaat Paşa
and then relayed to Wangenheim
who passed it on to Bethmann Hollweg
                    that *the Porte is intent*

on taking advantage of the World War
in order to make a clean sweep of internal enemies
— the indigenous Christians —
without being hindered in doing so
by diplomatic intervention from other countries[178]
over
1840   The Question
     to be addressed
     with the niceties
     that allies observe
as if someone had asked a Question
of someone
     who might
     then provide
     an answer
to the *Vali* Governor of Harpoot
1850   who was in no need of answers to The Question
     why all Armenians were to be
     marched along the road
     towards Dyarbekir
     along which *the deportations continued all summer*
     and throughout the fall of 1915.
     Several times the town crier announced
     that all Armenians could come out of their hiding places,
     as there would be no further deportations,
     and many of them were foolish enough to believe this,
1860   *with the results — not only once, but several times —*
     that when a goodly number of them were on the streets
     they were arrested,
     put in jail,
     and subsequently deported[179]
but not so far
from Mamouret-ul-Aziz town square,

where *there were perhaps 3,000 who left on that hot July day.*
The return soon afterwards
of the donkeys and mules which the Government had provided
1870   *indicated all too well*
the fate of those who had left[180]

         for the valleys along Lake Geoljuk's shore
         where the slaughtered were naked as morning rose,
         stripped in respect of the butcherer's lore
         that no merchant would buy blood-soaked
         clothes[181]

                 scavenged from the ten thousand bodies
                 America's Consul Davis estimated lay
         beside the lake.[182]

1880

He twice rode there from Mamouret-ul-Aziz,
along the Dyarbekir road
long before dawn
seeing *sufficient evidence*
to conclude
that the deportation
was to be understood
as annihilation[183]

     on which the missionary Henry Riggs was then obliged to take a strategy lesson
1890   from Harpoot MP Hadji Mehmet Effendi,
who told him that *the Armenians know what massacre is,*
and think they can bear that.
But let them see what deportation is.
They never dreamed of being deported.
They will soon learn
how much worse it is
than massacre,[184]

         for hate needs its story
         and hate crafts its truths,

1900
          while denial schemes a history
          in which the winners lose
once all is said and done
and the darkness has been lifted and the veil has been drawn
and the fear that men have
of the truth they learn each dawn
has become what they are
and must learn to be
and learn not to be
          there,

1910
          where it can be seen
          among the eucalyptus,
          smoke now,
where *Vali* Sabit Bey of Harpoot's
police scrawled *deportation* on the doors
in obeisance of the secret laws
Talat Paşa telegraphed as his crimes
while telling Morgenthau
          no Armenian can be our friend
          after what we have done to them,[185]

1920
          for hate needs its story
          and hate shapes its world,
          there, among the eucalyptus,
where *the famous 'revolution'*
was merely the determination
of the Armenians
to save their women's honour
and their own lives,[186]
          while the Caliphate was falling to the Cossacks
          and the Czarists were dug-in for the night,

1930
          when Sultan Mehmet got his news from the barracks:
          Gallipoli may fall at first light.

*

24 April 1915, Constantinople,
by when *the propaganda work necessary*
to justify an enormous crime
was fully prepared:
the Armenians had united with the enemy,
revolution was about to break out in Istanbul,
they were going to kill the Unionist leaders,
they were going to force open the Straits.[187]

1940   24 April 1915, Constantinople,
and the Turanian dream of the Young Turk trio[188]
is the life that is death the living alone know,
and words are monsters and dreams are false fate
faking the threat *not to exist as a state.*[189]

24 April 1915. Constantinople,
and America's Ambassador Morgenthau
reflected on the nightmare place he had known
in the time of the Pasha who made his vow:

We will not have the Armenians anywhere in Anatolia.
1950   *They can live in the desert but nowhere else.*[190]

So Aurora listened from the doorway of her house in Tchemesh-Gedzak
as her father questioned the horseman from Harpoot, who told them only

Ermenleri hep kesdiler — hep gitdi bitdi
the Armenians all killed — all gone, all dead.[191]

So Aurora watched in the square where her people had been gathered, and

there is only one God
Father Rhoupen began,
just as clearly as he could,
and with his eyes turned full upon the cruel officer.
1960   *He stopped for breath,*
and then went on —
and Jesus Christ, His Son, is my Saviour!

The officer drew his sword
and cut off Father Rhoupen's head.[192]

So Aurora heard how

Professor Poladian
told the officer
he would give his life
rather than deny

1970

his religion.
The soldier then
tore out his finger nails,
one by one,
and his toe nails
and pulled out his hair
and beard,
and then stabbed him
with knives
until he died.[193]

1980

and so

when this zaptieh and his companions
saw the young woman
was almost a mother
they took turns
running their bayonets
into her[194]

and so in Gwazim prison where her father and brother Paul were held

when it was dark the younger men,
who were strong and brave,

1990

killed all the older men
by hitting their heads
with the rocks Fatimeh had taken them.
Father killed Paul first,
because he was so little[195]

because it was better to die at the hands of family

74

than be butchered by the *zaptieh* police.

Better to die

Than be butchered

2000

Better to die

Than be butchered

Be

Butchered

2010 Be

Butchered

Be

only the screams now and then
of a girl who had attracted
some soldier's attention[196]
        and so
2020
                when children lagged behind,
                or got out of the line to rest,
                the zaptiehs
                would lift them on their bayonets
                and toss them away –
                sometimes trying to catch them again
                as they fell,
                on their bayonet points[197]
        and so

        and so

2030   and so
                   the soldiers of Nail Pasha,
                   the Vali of Diyarbekir
                   told with great enjoyment
                   how the bodies of little Armenian
                   children
                   had been mixed with cement
                   and built into the walls of the new
                   house
                   to fill the spaces

2040   *between the stones*[198]
                       I passed among
                       on my way
                       to Chapaghjur
                       that November evening
                when all had been forgotten
                when all was remembered
                when there were *no facts, only interpretations.*[199]

      Where
              nothing happened

2050   as
              my road was empty
      so
              I saw nothing
                    because Chapaghjur is Bingöl
                    now.
          There is no Chapaghjur
             so it has no road back to Diyarbekir.
               There is no road to Dyarbekir.
    There is a road to Dyarbekir I travelled one November morning.

2060   It was not a road I travelled
             from Chapaghjur to Diyarbekir.

It was not a road
There is no road.
There is no

Chapaghjur.
But there is a road to Diyarbekir
I travelled one cold November morning
From a place once named now disappeared
In propaganda and forgetting
Why all that was
Will always be
Travelling by that empty road
Across a land that is no more
Than all it was and today remains
An empty grave of rival claims
To truth and Being and the illusion borne of circumstance
That the life and death of this existence
Can be the life of which death alone makes sense.

*

But some spoke truth, when it was asked:
Why should we call ourselves
murderers?
Why have we taken on
this vast and difficult matter?
These things were done
to secure the future of our homeland,
which we know is greater
and holier
than even our own lives.[200]
So, the truth is horror, and horror is the truth.
Why then pretend?
Why deny,

2070

2080

2090

when all that can be known is truth
        and all that can be dreamed, the lie
        that is the empty road I passed by
that cold November morning,
south away from a place
where in June 1915 *in a loop of the river*
the thousands of dead bodies
created such a barrage
that the Euphrates
changed its course for about a hundred yards.[201]
                And the land remembers,
                as earth cradles its burden yet.
                The rivers know what they have carried,
                and the empty road cannot forget.

It makes no illusion,
winding south from where the *curling waters* of Armenia's Chapaghjur
were renamed the *thousand lakes* of Turkey's Bingöl town,
where I slept that cold November night[202]
among the ghosts that haunt in plain sight
                the illusion that what is wrong
                can become what is right
                when men hide the truth from truth.
Then they are trying to forget
that their hate needs its story.
True to themselves,
why deny?
Why pretend?
                They are the murderers.
Why deny?
Why pretend?
                They are the men of genocide – though this had
yet to become its name.

But why deny?
Why pretend?

2130   They are what men are,
                       as hate shapes its world.
                       There.
                       See it
                                among the eucalyptus.
                       It is smoke now,
        twisting through the emptiness of that road
                                I journeyed down that cold November morning
                                in the footsteps of a story I was told
                                would be silenced into myth and forgetting
2140   if that truth was hollowed out before it's sold
                       by the savage left to hide from his image
                       by the hand that holds the blade that is washed clean
                       as the Paşa, now feasting on the carnage,
                       sees beauty in all that is obscene.
                                People.
                                What is the number?
                                People.
                                The number.
                                People.
2150   People on the road
                       between a place that is no more and
                       the place where *every person sent into exile*
                       is considered by the government
                       as dead[203]
        to those who would have them dead
        but alive to every remembering soul
        who can see the truth when lies are bred
        by men who sell what others stole,
                                still, now, after this long century lived
2160   through times when death seemed life's obsession,

79

and truths and lies were like noise enslaved
by words mouthing an official version[204]
told and retold so many times as facts
that might one day become the make-believe
from which myths are made as stories weave
their way through time and into memory
where what cannot be believed is not believed
where what cannot be true cannot truly
be the horror that is made
2170 so *the word denial is used intentionally*
to prevent opposing discourse and consequently a debate,[205]
and because *Dr Justin McCarthy of the University of Louisville,*
calculates the actual losses as slightly less than 600,000[206]
and it can officially be stated that
a great portion of the Ottoman Armenians were not killed[207]
and so escaped the plans of Dr Bahaeddin Şakir Bey
who issued Talaat Paşa's annihilation order through the
Teşkilat-i Mahsusa Special Organization he established for the task.
And so
2180 *Armenian losses were few*
in comparison to the over 2.5 million Muslim
dead from the same period[209]
the official version states,
as if equanimity is to claim
that genocide is about debates
and cause of death is all the same,
while still the official version goes
that *no direct evidence has been discovered*
demonstrating that any Ottoman official
2190 *sought the destruction of the Ottoman Armenians as such.*[210]

As such.

80

As such, when all that Talaat Paşa wrote
to Diyarbekir, Urfa and Harpoot
        hid nothing.
Hate needs its story.
Hate shapes its world.
        There, see it among the eucalyptus
2200   beside the empty road
        from Chapaghjur,
        as Diyarbekir opens up beneath the cold
        November sky,
        and what became of what had happened
        became the savage truth of savage men,
        when Hitler asked his High Command:
        Wer redet heute noch von der Vernichtung der
        Armenier?[211]
Who still speaks today about the annihilation of the Armenians he mused,
2210   like a pupil who had learned a lesson
        and knew the answer to The Question.

7: Ulica Ofiar Faszyzmu 12

Henryk Mandelbaum

What it would be to call you by your name? You. What would be
and what would not? You. You are at 12. On a street. You exist
and do not. You are made, making, unmade. It is you. You stand.
You rest. You are in shadow. You change. You open. You close.
When you are called by your name will it be the last word? You eye,
mouth gaping, teeth mesh. It is to be invisible. All that is seen is
invisible because it is impossible. It is. And so it cannot be. The
language does not speak of it. The language cannot speak of it. But
everybody knew what to do without talking. Yet the revulsion remained. I didn't
want to pull the deceased by the hands, because the bodies had lain there quite
a while waiting to be burned and it sometimes happened that the skin came off
the hands like a glove.[212] It is. So it cannot be. *How did the other men*
react? The same as me. They saw themselves in those deceased. Did you
converse? About what? What subject did we have? Family? Escape? Freedom?
We had no subject. We were in hell.[213] It is this. It is invisible to all but
those who see. *We burned three people at a time in the furnace, and even*
four if they were thin, but seldom, because if a person was thin we put them off
to the side to add them to the fatter ones. A stout person burns like wood chips.
Just as there's sap in wood chips, there's fat in a person. Sometimes not
everything burned, and there were leg bones or bits of skull left. When you put
new bodies in, they caught fire immediately from the temperature. How long did

2220

2230

83

it take to reduce them to ashes? Fifteen to twenty minutes.[214] To ashes. Time
to ashes. It took time. Some time. *The ashes were removed from the
furnace and heaped up at the side. We ran ashes through a sieve until the bones
were as fine as salt. A truck came for these prepared ashes and took them to
the Vistula.*[215] Time as water. Water into day. Day into night. It is
not passing. Nothing passes. *No one except our Sonderkommando can
grasp what happened. Maybe only the stars at night. And the woods still
growing there today*[216] where the rings of a sawn stump date from that
time. They waited here. A breeze hushes the birches in their grove.
The birches hush in their grove. Sparrows in the high branches
follow a woodpecker from stump to bough shifting dapple sun in
shards that catch a yellow butterfly in its short flutter of life upon
the ashen memory of air. You exist and do not. You are invisible
because you are impossible. It is. And so it cannot be

Filip Müller

that when you are called by your name, all that must be said will
have been said. Tomorrow will be the day when all that is gone will
have woken on tomorrow. You are what you have become. You
are all that you were. You are all that had been imagined for you,
long before the time that you became. It is to imagine what can be
heard. It is what the dynamite left behind. Hands lay red brick.
Hands plier steel. Hands pour concrete. Hands place mesh. Hands
smooth walls. Hands screw bolts. Hands fix pipes. Hands attach
hooks. Hands paint red signs on pale blue walls. Feet pace. Hinges
swing. *Quiet as lambs they undressed…Each tried his or her best to hurry up
with their undressing so that they might be first to get under the shower…When
the last one had crossed the threshold, two SS men slammed shut the heavy
iron-studded door which was fitted with a rubber seal, and bolted it.*[217] Then

84

you beckon me into your old home. You lift your gaze, upward to where the birch-grove hums your name. We are breathing you as we walk. You are inside us. Your ash is inside us. We are your ash, the gift Oberscharführer Voss said must be prepared: *All you have to do is to see that every other load consists of two men and one woman from the transport, together with a Mussulman and a child. For every other load use only good material from the transport, two men, one woman and a child. After every two loadings empty out the ashes to prevent the channels from getting blocked*[218] and then *we would talk to them as if they were still alive, and even if there was no reply it appeared to worry no one, for we supplied our own answers*[219] while you taunt for your name to be spoken as your silence does its work. You are neither night nor day. Your silence does its work. You know we must fill your void. You wait for the sound of breath, than make it yours when the instruction is given *that the most economical and fuel-saving procedure would be to burn the bodies of a well-nourished man and an emaciated woman, or vice versa, together with that of a child, because as the experiments had established, in this combination, once they had caught fire, the dead would continue to burn without any further coke being required*[220] where the birches hum in their grove and sparrows in the high branches follow a woodpecker from stump to bough shifting in the dapple-sun shards that catch a yellow butterfly in its short flutter of life upon that air, where what exists does not exist and what cannot be seen is invisible. We breathe your air. We are in your house.

Top Secret

Meyer Neumann Bühler Klopfer Eichmann Lange Luther Leibbrandt Stuckart Freisler Heydrich Kritzinger Hoffman Schöngarth Müller. Another possible solution of the problem has now taken the place of emigration, i.e. the evacuation of the Jews to the East, provided that the Führer gives the appropriate approval in advance. These actions are, however, only to be considered provisional, but practical experience is already being collected which is of the greatest importance in relation to the future final solution of the Jewish question. Approximately 11 million Jews will be involved in the final solution of the European Jewish question. The number of Jews given here for foreign countries includes, however, only those Jews who still adhere to the Jewish faith, since some countries still do not have a definition of the term 'Jew' according to racial principles. The handling of the problem in the individual countries will

2300 *meet with difficulties due to the attitude and outlook of the people there, especially in Hungary and Rumania. Under proper guidance, in the course of the final solution the Jews are to be allocated for appropriate labour in the East. Able-bodied Jews, separated according to sex, will be taken in large work columns to these areas for work on roads, in the course of which action doubtless a large portion will be eliminated by natural causes. The possible final remnant will, since it will undoubtedly consist of the most resistant portion, have to be treated accordingly, because it is the product of natural selection and would, if released, act as the seed of a new Jewish revival (see the experience of history.) In the course of the practical execution of the final solution, Europe will be*

2310 *combed through from west to east. Germany proper, including the Protectorate of Bohemia and Moravia, will have to be handled first due to the housing problem and additional social and political necessities. The evacuated Jews will first be sent, group by group, to so-called transit ghettos, from which they will be transported to the East. In the course of the final solution plans, the Nuremberg Laws should provide a certain foundation, in which a prerequisite for the absolute solution of the problem is also the solution to the problem of mixed marriages and persons of mixed blood. State Secretary Dr. Bühler stated that the General Government would welcome it if the final solution of this problem could be begun in the General Government, since on the one hand transportation*

2320 *does not play such a large role here nor would problems of labor supply hamper this action. Jews must be removed from the territory of the General Government as quickly as possible, since it is especially here that the Jew as an epidemic carrier represents an extreme danger and on the other hand he is causing permanent chaos in the economic structure of the country through continued black market dealings. Moreover, of the approximately 2 1/2 million Jews concerned, the majority is unfit for work. He had only one request, to solve the Jewish question in this area as quickly as possible. In conclusion the different types of possible solutions were discussed, during which discussion both Gauleiter Dr. Meyer and State Secretary Dr. Bühler took the position that certain preparatory activities for the final solution should be carried out immediately in the territories in question, in which process alarming the populace must be avoided.*[221]

George Steiner

Those who speak must be silent. Those who are silent cannot speak. The living do not have the language, while those who are silent are saying all that can be said, sensing – knowing – that the *problem as to whether there is a human form of language adequate to the conceptualisation and understanding of Auschwitz, as to whether the limits of language do not fall short of the limits of the Shoah-experience, is now ineradicably installed in Jewish existence*[222] as we try to speak of it. To speak its name. To say its name, and the *remembrancer*[223]drifts among the ghosts and ash, asking in the silence: *What categories of intelligibility, what grammar of reason, indeed what vocabulary in the most concrete sense, can incorporate, can articulate, can give interpretation to, the abyss of 1938-45*[224] whose rust tracks now await its trucks to pass along the branch line from Oświęcim? Is this an aftermath, where this remembrancer stands? Is this an aftermath, when *Niemand bespricht unsern Staub? No-one bespeaks our dust*[225] that is the memory. *No one conjures our dust*[226] that is the nothing we have become. *No-one incants our dust*[227] that is the no-thing of wordlessness you inflict as a second death, conspired in *that greatest lie, which is forgetting.*[228] Is this an aftermath, or the place where *Niemand knetet uns wieder aus Erde und Lehm*[229] whose cry is voiced in every step that grinds beneath these footsteps along the ashen promenade: *No one moulds us again out of earth and clay*, with the remembrancer cast into the wordlessness you inflict. Your silence has done its work, leaving one to fill the void with the word you know cannot be breathed. You know why the grass grows lush among the meadow glades where the birch and poplar do not stoop to shadow. You know what lies beneath those lush blades that mark *that realm of potential –*

2360 *now realised – human bestiality, or, rather, abandonment of the human and regression to bestiality, which both precedes language, as it does in the animal, and comes after language as it does in death*[230] that is a place now. Death lives here, where you taunt the remembrancer as he torments himself with the possibility that *to try to speak or write intelligibly, interpretatively, about Auschwitz is to misconceive totally the nature of that event and to misconstrue totally the necessary constraints of humanity within language*[231] as, in his mourning, we hear him ask: *Is the poet's voice not an insult to the naked cry?*[232]

Inferno

I breathe wire. You are watching. You see my fear. You smell me.
2370 You brought me here, and now you watch me where I stand in *a meagre ray of sunlight*[233] at the top of the steps from whose cellar darkness you beckon. This is where you took them, after you were betrayed by your Confessor.[234] This is where you took them, after your *spirit, which in matters of belief had up to then been so peacefully and surely shepherded, had been severely shaken and the deep, genuine faith of a child had been shattered.*[235] You are this place where *the weeping puts an end to weeping, and the grief that finds no outlet from the eyes turns inward to intensify the anguish.*[236] And what do you see now in this place you made, even as *Jew-hatred, together with the more general and even deeper-*

2380 *lying resentment of monotheism and sacrificial morality, took on their terrible, festering virulence precisely as Christianity and a belief in God as such began receding from the spiritual habits and intellectual-political adherence of Western civilization?*[237] You have no answer, and instead gouge your story from its hollow as you ponder your Sonderkommando slaves whose *eagerness with which they carried out their duties never ceased to amaze me*[238] as *they carried out all these tasks with a callous indifference as though it were part of an ordinary day's work*[239] they tortured through at every touch under the whip-hand of you who are no-thing. You gouge your story from its hollow, word your lines and know you are an

2390 absence. You are the one whose presence is an absence. You are no-thing, whose *strength in the executive lay not in creative action, but in our complete supervision*[240] at the hands of that utopia you stoke in the *bierkeller* flames you feign to capture in a pretence of knowing that *all were judged according to what they had done. Then Death and Hades were thrown into the lake of fire. This is the second death, the lake of fire, and anyone whose name was not found written in the book of life was thrown into the lake of fire.*[241] But you know it would be you they judge. So you burn the book, the nameless then as nameless as the names you skinned in your revenge on that Confessor who shamed that child by its truth

2400 that is the flames of those you *gathered in the pit,*[242] those you stole from a story you envied perhaps had once been yours, and nod sagely as your slaves explain that *by digging a channel which sloped slightly to either side from the centre point, it would be possible to catch the fat exuding from the corpses as they were burning in the pit, in two collecting pans at either end of the channel…a drain channel to catch human fat which in turn would be used as fuel*[243]

Rudolf Höss

beneath where the birches hum in their grove and a sparrow flits from stump to bough *under the blossom-laden fruit trees of the Cottage*

2410 *orchard*[244] under the blossom-laden fruit trees of the Cottage orchard under the blossom-laden fruit trees of the Cottage orchard the Cottage orchard the Cottage orchard the Cottage orchard where *during the spring of 1942 hundreds of vigorous men and women walked all unsuspecting to their deaths in the gas chambers, under the blossom-laden fruit trees of the Cottage orchard,* though in July 1942 *the gypsies were first to be separated from the others, as with the Jews*[245] and *though it was not easy to drive them into the gas chambers…they were as trusting as children,*[246] *my best-loved prisoners, if I may put it that way*[247] on looking back to gouge the story from its hollow and reflect on the *richly varied life of a*

2420 *concentration camp*[248] where the *dog handlers when they were bored, or wanted to have some fun, would set their dogs on the prisoners*[249] over whom *I had never anticipated being made a Kommandant so quickly, especially as some very senior protective custody camp commanders had been waiting a long time for a commandant's post to fall vacant*[250] though when it did *I was no longer happy in Auschwitz once the mass extermination had begun*[251] as *it was certainly an extraordinary and monstrous order* though *the reasons behind the extermination seemed to me right*[252] extermination seemed to me right extermination seemed to me right seemed to me right seemed to me right seemed to me right that *the Jews in Auschwitz…knew, without*

2430 *exception, that they were condemned to death, that they would live only so long as they could work…they no longer had the will to live, everything had become a matter of indifference to them…sooner or later death was inevitable, I firmly maintain*[253] I firmly maintain I firmly maintain I firmly maintain *during this first experience of gassing people I did not fully realise what was happening, perhaps because I was too impressed by the whole procedure*[254] which had first been tested successfully on the captured Russian soldiers,[255] and *I must even admit that this gassing set my mind at rest, for the mass extermination of the Jews was to start soon and at that time neither Eichmann nor I was certain how these mass killings were to be carried*

2440 *out…now we had the gas, and we had established the procedure*[256] and it *could be observed through the peep-hole in the door that those who were standing nearest to the induction vents were killed at once…those who screamed and those who were old or sick or weak, or the small children, died quicker than those who were healthy or young*[257] whose *ashes were taken in lorries to the Vistula, where they immediately drifted away and dissolved*[258] while I and I and I and I and I *in Auschwitz I truly had no reason to complain that I was bored*[259] as I as I as I could watch from the window of the children's room from where the gas chamber and crematorium of Auschwitz 1 was visible through the birch leaves, and, Oh, said the Kommandant's maid Danuta, *at home, Höss was ideal. He loved the children. He liked to lie down with them on the sofa in their room. He kissed them, caressed them, and talked to them in a lovely way*[260]

Private Lives

yes, *talked to them in a lovely way* in the house from where the children could see the gas chamber and the crematorium beyond the birch leaf shadow cast across the evening 'Onkel Heini' came to visit and *took Höss's children on his knee.* 'Onkel Heini' the children called, as Onkel *chatted cordially* with the Kommandant and to the *children on his knee.* Ah, yes, 'Onkel Heini'. 'Heini'. 'Heinrich'. 'Onkel' Heinrich. Heinrich. Reichsführer Heinrich. Reichsführer Heinrich. Himmler. 'Onkel' Himmler. SS-Reichsführer Himmler with the *Höss's children on his knee* taking sugar with his tea, sugar from the store *well stocked at this time because it also stored food products confiscated from Jews arriving in Auschwitz in mass transports, sent from those transports directly to the gas for the most part*[261] so that Onkel Heini could take his tea. And there are the Wöntzes, neighbours, SS-Unterscharsführer Wöntz and his wife, *simple folk. In their small garden they grew vegetables and raised chickens. It was at their house that I first saw such beautiful jewellery, and so much of it…brooches, necklaces, watches and earrings,*[262] and there the house of SS-Sturmbannführer Bischoff – the man who

2470 built the crematoria and the gas chambers – and here is the gold his wife owned and which their maid Maria would wonder at,[263] and over there the home of SS-Hauptscharführer Palitzsch, whose housemaid Helena had heard he was the executioner at the Death Wall in the courtyard of Block 11: *and when I learned what a figure of fear Palitzsch was in the camp, I couldn't believe it. At home he was the best of men. He treated me well. He loved his children madly,*[264] yes, *loved his children madly*, just like SS-Oberscharführer Kalaus, who Bogusława Głowacka still remembers from her days in service at the house from *where it was impossible not to see the unloading of the transports. Corpses*

2480 *were collected each morning after each transport. Kalaus sent his family away. Long before this, Frau Kalaus took the more valuable things – I think they came from the camp – to her family home*[265] just like the wife of SS-Obersturmführer Albert where Halina Lekacz worked in that sparse apartment where *Frau Albert, who had nothing when I started working for them, came into the possession of jewellery and several rings*[266] brought as lovely gifts by her generous husband; fine men, these husbands, caring as the *homebody* SS-Haupsturmführer Fischer, who Aleksandra Stawarczyk watched in the kitchen at his main task: peeling potatoes cooked in their skins when he came home on the

2490 dot of 1 o'clock for lunch – every day at 1 o'clock, before he went back to work. Went back to work with a fond farewell. A hand bids a fond farewell. A hand bids a fond farewell as he returns to work at the ramp, directing *Men to the left Women to the right?*[267] Men to the left Women to the right Men to the left Women to the right Men to the left Women to the right. *Eight words spoken quietly, indifferently, without emotion. Eight simple, short words*[268] and a hand that bade a fond farewell. A hand to the right. To the right. To the right. To the right along the ashen promenade, then home again for the evening concert *on the little square between the Kommandant's office and the*

2500 *crematorium.*[269]

I want the world to read and to resolve that this must never, never be permitted to happen again[270] as you wait to wait as you haunt the shadow where the birch bough bows. You are felt here. Cannot be seen. Shadow. Where the bough stoops as the doctor in his uniform. To the right. To the left. A hand gestured to the right. A hand gestured to the left and *I put my little boy on the left side. With my stupid love. I told the truth that he was not yet twelve years old. I wanted to spare him from the forced labour, and with this I killed him.*[271] And *this must never, never be permitted to happen again* as the Czech boy, *who was in love with a young Vertreterin from our camp, said good-bye to her through the barbed wire that separated us. He knew how the day would end for him. When you see the first flames from the crematorium at day-break,* he said, *you will know that is my greeting to you*[272] and that life is death and death is daylight and daylight is infernal and the inferno is *Irma Griese coming from the Führerstube, her whip in hand, to designate the next batch for the gas chamber*[273] which is no mystery, no rumour, no doubt. No doubt who had been chosen. Chosen. Chosen. Selected, *when a cord was stretched to a certain height. All who passed under this mark were automatically set aside for the gas chambers. Of one hundred children, only five or six survived*[274] survived survived survived survived. Five or six? Perhaps it was six. Perhaps six survived. Not five but six. And did you look closely at that sixth child from your watchtower among the birches, where you resolved that this must be permitted to happen again and again and again, until the work is done? Is done. Because only then could it never happen again. Is it done? Only when the work is done will it *never be permitted to happen again*, you whisper where you watch from the wire in which you cage the ones who whisper wondering to this day if the work you've done is done among the mothers, daughters and younger sons who are the work that will be done, the work that will

93

2530   be done. Thy Will Be Done, till all is said and done. And gone. From the place where a sun once shone, where now the light and dark are one.

Viktor E Frankl

It spoke. To it. This night. It. Sound. Sounds spoke. Shape. Smell. It. It. Something beyond. With. In. With. Known. It. Know it within. Know. It. Within. It spoke. To it. Another moaned. Stop that moaning. Stop that sound. Stop. That. Sound. Of. That. Man. That man. That. Man. Beside it on the voyage from where it calls, from where *I shall never forget how I was roused one night by the groans of a fellow prisoner who threw himself about in his sleep, obviously having a*

2540   *horrible nightmare. Since I had always been especially sorry for people who suffered from fearful dreams or deliria, I wanted to wake the poor man. Suddenly I drew back my hand which was ready to shake him, frightened at the thing I was about to do. At that moment I became intensely conscious of the fact that no dream, no matter how horrible, could be as bad as the reality of the camp which surrounded us and to which I was about to recall him*[275] from where it called inside its night. It is night, and the night voice spoke of what could once be seen beyond its night. Beyond. And then the one and then the other and then the time they passed together. And then the. Then that. Then it. A memory. Of another. Far off. Where

2550   there is what was before. Where there is all that will come. When this has passed and is the past. Then there will be meaning. Here. Here. This night. This night, here, now. It spoke. Words screamed into the night by the man on his night voyage. Words without meaning. This place is no meaning. Death is this. The living with no meaning. To live without meaning. Death is this. This death. This is death. Death is its meaning, so *what was really needed was a fundamental change in our attitudes towards life. We had to learn ourselves and, furthermore, we had to teach the despairing men, that it did really not matter what we expected from life, but rather what life expected from us. We needed to stop asking about the meaning of life, and instead to think of ourselves as those who were being questioned by life – daily and hourly*[276] where there are no days nor hours. Only movement. Between the terror and the terror that is the truth of the meaning. The truth of knowing that *the prisoner who lost faith in the future – his future – was doomed. With his loss of faith in the future, he also lost his spiritual hold…We all feared this moment – not for ourselves, but for our friends…He simply gave up. There he remained, lying in his own excreta, and nothing bothered him anymore.*[277]

Paul Celan

He spoke of it this night, this place where *the word is a word torn from silence*[278] by stuttered breath that steps and steps from self into the world to which it. Speaks. Speaks. Speaks the place from which it came, of the sound of its *rebellion against silence,*[279] its *exit from the self,*[280] its role *not in its meaning but in its invoking*[281] in the stuttered speak of words the poet breath-breathes breath-breathes until the turn and turning into all that can be said that cannot be more than can be said in *the crystal of the poetic word*[282] he, poet, heard breathe from the place whose name is one *for which language has found no word.*[283] That is the place where the poem was born. That is its day. The 20th of January 1942. All was agreed in ninety minutes *Am Großen Wannsee 56–58,* that *der Tod ist ein Meister aus Deutschland*[284] whose torture is that master of the breath spoken in which *tongue his parents and millions of fellow Jews had been butchered,*[285] that tongue that tastes the black milk we drink at night we drink at noon[286] and speak of through starless night, for *die Nacht braucht keine Sterne, nirgends fragt es nach dir.*[287] No, *the night needs no stars. Nowhere does anyone ask for you* where there is no one who knows to ask after the one who is left to ask after those who are now gone among the yellow fragments of the stars that are the hollow mirror of the place which knows *the place where they lay, it has a name – it has none.*[288] None. None. It has none. No name that can be spoken *in that tongue* in which to name would be to say. You. To say is to name. You. To breathe you is the turn of you from breath to life in the word of you in the language of the *Meister aus Deutschland* who skinned the names and turned the stars to rags *verbracht ins Gelände mit der untrüglichen Spur*[289] beside tracks where a gesture now is to the right a gesture now is to the left *men to the left women to the right. Eight words spoken quietly, indifferently, without emotion. Eight simple, short words. Yet that was the moment when I left my mother...I didn't know that this was the moment in time and the place where I was leaving my mother and Tzipora forever. I kept walking, my father holding my hand*[290] holding a hand holding a hand *into the terrain with the unmistakable track*[291] where the birches hum in their grove and a sparrow flits from stump to bough shifting in the dapple-sun that catches the yellow butterfly in its passing upon the *Asche. Asche, Asche. Nacht. Nacht-und-Nacht. – Zum Aug geh, zum feuchten*[292] whose gaze we catch in the house of *Ash. Ash, ash. Night. Night-and-night. – Go to the eye, the moist one* watching from the dead of heaven over those *driven into the terrain with the unmistakable track: Grass. Grass, written asunder.*[293]

Shlomo Venezia

We came back out of the Crematorium, but instead of turning right to go back to the barracks, they made us turn left, through the little forest of birches. I'd never seen this kind of tree in Greece, but in Birkenau they were the only trees one saw surrounding the camp. As we walked along the path, all we could hear was the wind whistling through the silvery leaves[294] that are the hushing of the grove gagged in its voltage hem taut as eyelid skin. Barbed thorn. *Adonai* blazed in the rise of murmur. *Adonai* blazed among the silver leaves, barbed thorn jagging the throat of the little white house when all the people went inside, and the hospital truck brought a man who climbed on a stool to reach the shaft and poured from his can then shut the opening. Then left, though *the shouts and crying had not stopped, and they redoubled in intensity after a few minutes. This lasted for ten or twelve minutes, then silence*[295] that is the hushing grove in the growing season that sucks the ash you feed to fruit the furnace of your womb that bore the offspring you cradle in your flames that are the darkness of this summer day in the *Cottage orchard under the blossom-laden fruit trees* where the Sonderkommando slaves of Höss numb life to dead moments *well aware that once the actions were completed they, too, would meet exactly the same fate as that suffered by these thousands of their own race, to whose destruction they had contributed so greatly. Yet the eagerness with which they carried out their duties never ceased to amaze me* as *they carried out all these tasks with a callous indifference as though it were part of an ordinary day's work*[296] you tortured them to live as men who *didn't think of anything – we couldn't exchange a single word. Not because it was forbidden, but because we were terror-struck. We had turned into robots, obeying orders while trying not to think, so we could survive for a few hours longer*[297] as tormented souls your coward taunts along *der untrüglichen Spur*[298] whose cry is voiced in every step that grinds the ashen promenade to where the iron tracks bind our lives in this horror that is *Life. Since then I've never had a normal life. I've never been able to pretend that everything was all right and go off dancing, like others, without a care in the world…Everything takes me back to the camp. Whatever I do, whatever I see, my mind keeps harking back to that same place. It's as if the 'work' I was forced to do there had never really left my head…Nobody ever really gets out of the Crematorium.*[299]

Elie Wiesel

No, *the night needs no stars. Nowhere does anyone ask for you*[300] nowhere does anyone ask for you nowhere does anyone ask for you in the whisper Word chant-mesmerised to memory of what had gone before the morning came[301] that is yesterday become today on the *Asche. Asche, Asche. Nacht. Nacht-und-Nacht*[302] that is the Night of

2650   what was whispered when night star was the comfort of eternity the morning star the passing night a whisper mesmerised to memory that *Yisgadal, veyiskadash, shmey raba…may His name be celebrated and sanctified…*[303] where now *nirgends fragt es nach dir*[304] *nirgends fragt es nach dir nirgends fragt es nach dir* where *the night needs no stars* where *nowhere does anyone ask for you* once God chose to be silent[305] and the moment came to prayer the moment to prayer the moment with the recitation the recitation child chant-mesmerised to memory to memory to memory in one who once had been the boy believer[306] but where there is no one who knows to ask after

2660   the one who is left to ask after those who are now gone among the yellow fragments of the stars that are the hollow mirror of the place which knows *the place where they lay, it has a name – it has none*[307] and the names of those who had gone are not mentioned[308] those who do not ask of them those who do not ask of them those who are became the shadow[309] Mrs Schächter warned of in her vision[310] warned of on the journey warned of in her nightmare warned of on the fattened light the transport delivered to the flames that night that *needs no stars*[311] to image what once was cast heavenward in devoted recitation cast to memory to memory to memory in what

2670   once had been the young boy believer[312] who no longer prayed[313] in that whisper mesmerised to memory of what had gone before the first light of dawn[314] that is yesterday become today on the *Asche. Asche, Asche. Nacht. Nacht-und-Nacht*[315] that is light is dark is light as the darkness of the milk we drink as black as white at daybreak under flaming night and *the blossom-laden fruit trees of the Cottage orchard*[316] where *modern barbarism sprang in some intimate, perhaps necessary way from the very core and locale of humanistic civilization*[317] and the boy who held his father's hand[318] held a hand held a hand held a hand held a hand knowing only that he was alone[319] in this place *where the house of civilization proved no shelter*[320] where at night the soup tasted of corpses[321]

2680

Primo Levi

until the morning, *when it seemed as though the new sun rose as an ally of our enemies to assist in our destruction*[322] beneath the window of the children's room in the house where Frau Höss lingers secret tristes with *Häftling* prisoner Böhner[323] while her absent Kommandant ejaculates his ashen flame, and recalls must ask his neighbour: *That corpse you planted last year in your garden, Has it begun to sprout? Will it bloom this year? Or has the sudden frost disturbed its bed? O keep the Dog far hence, that's friend to men, Or with his nails he'll dig it up again*[324] and again and again into this eternity of empty wind torn to fleshen rags through the barb of teeth that flay the roll-call hollow storm when *for the first time we become aware that our language lacks words to express this offence, the demolition of man*[325] whose clog steps crush the ash that feeds its beast, the beast, the beast that feeds, that eats the beast that feeds what comes its way. Its way. It. Its. It. It. It is. It is. You. You. You are it. You are it. You are its. Name. The name. The name. You are. You are the word of it. There is no word *for which language has found no word*[326] but hell. *Today, in our times, hell must be like this*[327] place that has been made for time to pass *drop by drop*[328] while *above us the malevolent clouds chase each other to separate us from the sun*[329] set rise set rise set rise on Selection. Day. Selection Day. The selection that is day and night and day and night. And day. And night when *we spoke of everything without ever mentioning those who had disappeared*[330] into the silence known by silence where *nirgends fragt es nach dir*[331] in payment of *an old debt*[332] the Kommandant collects in the *Häftlinge* skins[333] of the tormented ones who fight *with all our strength to prevent the arrival of winter*[334] time which passes *drop by drop* towards the wisdom of *not trying to understand, not imagining the future, not tormenting ourselves as to how and when it would all be over; not asking others or ourselves any questions*[335] which may lead to the mistake of trying to make sense, of trying to explain, of trying to explain what can only be explained by never seeking to explain how aglitter in her stolen gold Frau Höss could sit so long in secret triste with *Häftling* Böhner[336] in her pavilion shade beside the wire while husband Kommandant steps away from the peep-hole trance and turning to his neighbour asks: *That corpse you planted last year in your garden, Has it begun to sprout*

Miklós Nyiszli

into the specimens you have destined for alcoholic preservation at the *Kaiser Wilhelm-Institut für Anthropologie, Menschliche Erblehre und Eugenik* to where *these parts were specially packed to be sent through the mail, stamped 'War Material – Urgent', they were given top priority in transit*[337] the father and son with rickets and a deformed right foot, who Doctor Mengele ordered *must not be cremated. They must be preserved and their skeletons sent to the Anthropological Museum in Berlin. What system do you know for the preparation of skeletons? There are two methods: immersing the bodies in lime chloride then in a gasoline bath, which dissolves all the fat and makes the skeletons dry, odourless and white. Then there's the second method: by cooking. Dr Mengele ordered me to use the*

2690

quickest method: by cooking[338] and then give them *top priority in transit* for earnest examination by Doctor Fischer, Doctor Fischer and the Directors, *who always warmly thanked Dr Mengele for this rare and precious material* selected by a tilt of the hand from those *whose faces, bloated and blue, were so deformed as to be almost unrecognisable. Nevertheless some of the Sonderkommando did recognise their kin*[339] among the flesh and hair, *did recognise their kin did recognise their kin did recognise* their children mothers brothers kin whose eyes beseeched whose lips begged words that could not would not must not speak of it that could not word its name but in the *naked cry*[340] of fire that brought the agony to an end when, *during the night our comrades had been taken to a nearby forest and killed by flame throwers. The Sonderkommando – thirteenth in the history of the crematoriums – had thus been annihilated*[341] so the silence could be total, the sole witnesses now crawling ashen Vistula's flow as the Doctors unwrapped the *Urgent* mail, wrenched gold melted into ingots, and Oberscharführer Mußfeld angrily denied the slaughter made his heart-beat race and blamed the booze instead,[342] yes, blamed the booze instead, yes, that's what gets the pulse rate up, *your diagnosis is incorrect. It doesn't bother me any more to kill a hundred men than it does to kill five. If I'm upset, it's merely because I drink too much* the ex-baker bragged to Doctor prisoner Nyiszli, fresh from shooting an orderly line of eighty men with the pistol now holstered at his hip, but *If I'm upset, it's merely because I drink too much* he snarled, and Nyiszli, in his silence: *If by chance I ever get out of this place alive, and have a chance to relate all I've seen and lived through, who will believe me*[343]

Martin Heidegger

even when the knowing is come *that the world's darkening never reaches to the light of Being,*[344] when the knowing is come that *we are too late for*

101

the gods and too early for Being, when the knowing is come *that Being's poem, just begun, is man* to whom the knowing has come that *he who thinks greatly must err greatly* in his timely *Zeit* and worldly *Sein* with the yellow butterfly among the mountain arnica *die gelbe Schmetterling unter der Arnika Montana* we shall name as *Wolfsfluch* Wolf's Bane *wenn sich der Schmetterling an einem Sommertag auf der Blume und den Flügeln niederläßt, yes, when on a summer's day the butterfly settles on the flower and, wings closed, sways with it in the meadow-breeze,*[345] then the folkloric fantasy you see awake will cast your darkness into your own black light[346] in time with the knowing in timely *Zeit* and worldly *Sein* your Führer screams is the one true path[347] to reach the cloudless peak above the orchids, so *wir können den Schritt nach hinten wagen der Philosophie in das Denken des Seins, sobald wir mit der Herkunft des Denkens vertraut geworden sind,*[348] yes, there *we may venture the step back out of philosophy into the thinking of Being as soon as we have grown familiar with the provenance of thinking* until *das Sprichwort des Denkens würde stillstehen sein Sein nur durch Unfähigwerden das sagen, was bleiben muß unausgesprochen* to *being only by becoming unable to say that which must remain unspoken* and wordless and un-Being and no-thing and no-time and no awakening into the silence silence silence, when the end lies at the heart of folkloric Being, you ask,[349] like the one who went before, the Chorus stepping between the scenes to say of Man: *he forges on, now to his destruction now again to greatness*[350] for all his thousands thousands thousands years when it was *the city cast out that man who weds himself to inhumanity,* and protests: *never share my hearth never think my thoughts whoever does such things*[351] – until now, now, at ashen time, now, as the Führer crafts Death from Life in the classroom of the Albert-Ludwigs-Universität Freiburg and *die Wahrheit wird euch frei Machen* this Rector tells the ones who will come to Be: *do not let theorems and ideas be the rules of your Being. The Führer himself and alone is the present and future German reality and its law*[352] the *present and future* reality as the Rector of Todtnauberg hut *weds himself to inhumanity* in a *silence both safeguarding and trying to*

2730

2740

2750

transcend the limits of speech which are, as in the very name of that hut, also those of death,[353] stars scattered *Sternwürfel drauf*[354] on the water of the well,

Theodor W Adorno

hollow as the ragged yellowing of the stars the night no longer can believe in words that are the truth to be believed now *die Nacht braucht keine Sterne*[355] now *the night needs no stars* which perhaps may have shone where then no light could bring to light what death was making then of life, *that the philosopheme of pure identity is death,*[356] yes, that the pure life is death, here, *where absolute negativity is in plain sight and ceased to surprise anyone,*[357] here where the ragged wings of butterfly scuttle charred red brick where the light cannot light what is clocked midday what is clocked in night in day by date by time that is an ever since, an ever since from *fearing death means fearing worse than death*[358] beneath the *birken* shade where it is a step away, a step here and there along the ashen promenade, while *above us the malevolent clouds chase each other to separate us from the sun*[359] which burns the ashen footsteps and wait for you as evening falls on these dark walls that will forever be the prison of the *one who escaped by accident, one who by rights should have been killed*[360] the one who *by way of atonement will be plagued by dreams such as that he is no longer living at all, that he was sent to the ovens in 1944 and his whole existence has been imaginary*[361] in the words that may perhaps imagine may be written into memory as the warning that what has happened cannot happen, cannot happen, cannot be, cannot be the *Being* that may once have been and perhaps was not because it cannot be that *Being* is its death, its death the life of *Being* suckled on your *black milk*[362] in time within the wire *wenn sich der Schmetterling an einem Sommertag auf der Blume und den Flügeln niederläßt,* yes, *when on a summer's day the butterfly settles on the flower and, wings closed, sways with it in the meadow-breeze*[363] that burns the ashen footsteps as evening falls on these dark walls that will forever be the prison where you will cage us in your wire where you will drag us to your gallows where you will plague us with your name that will always be the one who tells that *the sadism latent in everyone unerringly divines the weakness latent in everyone,*[364] that chokes the river's flowing ash your slaves scrape from the flames your angels blow *in the place where the nightmare of childhood has come true.*[365]

2790   The place that is you. It is you. It is you. You are Auschwitz.

8: El Dorado

I, Pedro de Cieza de León,
subject of Charles, my Trastámara king,
son of Llerena where no fortune was born

that year 1520 one day in spring
to my father Lopé mother Leonor,
God-fearing poor under Erasmus' wing,

2800   whose deviance shocked Extramadura
as heresy threatened God the true king
under the eye of our Inquisitor,[366]

I, Pedro de Cieza de León,
have heard it said of Guadalquivir
this river is heaving with bullion

moored at Sanlúcar de Barrameda[367]
then brought on the tide as far as Seville
2810   where now I go by *Via Argenta*[368]

this day in April 1535
to board *Cifuentes* for Cartagena
as *conquistador* scribe who no man alive

will say was one who thirsted for silver
but craved just to see *el Nuevo Mundo*
and witness my people as *cronista*

2820   of these golden times I was born into.
And now, our galleon in full sail,
we breast the writhing hunch of ocean's tow

drenched halyards wrenched as the fair winds wail
and we ride the waves on the skin of the surf
and leave the Old World to tell its old tale

behind us in homes where all that was safe
has faded like dreams when daybreak is come.
2830   Llerena is gone, and all that I crave

is the years are as kind as I would treat them,
and my *compañeros* be good men
who know all they do is done but for Him.

*

Forty-five days at sea, we drop anchor
where Captain Pedro de Heredia[369]
struck land in the bay now our open door

to the lands and tales of wonder and fear
2840   of what lay along Sinú's forest banks.
We dream that the Southern Ocean is near,

fed by the waters that carry these ranks
our Captain Alonso de Cáceres now leads,

I as his page boy expecting no thanks

more than to reach the coast Sinú's stream feeds
beyond the *Cordillera de los Andes*,
there where the gold of El Dorado seeds

2850

the land I travel with God as my witness.
So it is, two years by *Río Verde*
to *Antioquía* across *los llanos*

by the salt route we *conquistadores* pray
will lead to the golden palace we dreamed
awaits our coming by the end of this day,

as the land we march becomes one we have turned

2860

from fields that feed where the maize crops grow
to the hunger of dust where the fields have burned,

when the call comes from Marquis Pizarro
to save Peru for God and Spain, there
I with my Captain Jorge Robledo

entered the empire of the Inca,
where Spain's men feasted on each other's feuds
and I joined the bandits of Belalcázar.[370]

2870

Why so, I have not time to tell in words.
He beheaded my Captain Jorge Robledo
when as such men do they spoke with swords,

then we crossed the river Angasmayo
stepped into Peru by *rumi chaca*[371]
and heard the first sounds of *Tahuantinsuyu*.[372]

To know what I see before my own eyes
I must know of all that went before me,
2880   of lives once led before the golden prize

was dreamed by gallants thirsting for glory.
To know of good one must witness the sins
of the tyrant in all his cruelty,

so thundered the Bishop of Chiapas
whose name is forever carved in this stone,
Fray Bartolomé de las Casas,

2890   in whose footsteps I follow as my own,
this *Protectoría de los Indios*,
like no other Spaniard who left his home

to witness the looting *compañeros*
in their savage search for El Dorado.
His name resounds along the Royal Roads

I now ride as scribe and *conquistador*
who, like St Isidore's *historein*,[373]
2900   speaks not of what's heard but all that I saw

of Belalcázar and all of his kind,
who burned alive the great Indian lords
in Quito, and stole what gold they could find[374]

then heeded the call and sharpened their swords
to fight Spain's rebels defying their King,

then plunder the lands and shackle the hordes,

2910 whose lives I see now as we are passing
along the ruins of this Royal Road,
are starved of food by armies advancing

whose slaves once farmers now carry our loads
and die before us from sickness and thirst
in a land where once great Inca had strode.

I wonder if truth is a land now cursed
to die before my never-sleeping eyes,
2920 or if my witness – neither last nor first –

is illusion men will later call lies,
as I scribe my notes of horror and crimes
we Spaniards commit but no law denies.

Now twelve years have passed since those distant times
of my first steps on *el Nuevo Mundo*,
since when that boy is the man who became

2930 the witness whose pen writes the truth you will know
of how a people came to disappear
from the very earth they would plough and sow

with no suspicion there was danger near
that they were the last Inca, victims of
the greed of most or all of us here.[375]

They will be wiped out completely. This truth
has been known since Atahualpa was tricked
2940 into stuffing his rooms with gold to the roof

in return for promises melted as bricks
of gold that dazzled *conquistador* homes
while Inca was burned on a pyre of sticks.

Garrotted and burned to his blackened bones,
Atahualpa honoured his ransom promise,
but was naïve like one who never learns

2950   all the world's gold won't satisfy pirates,
and now, *through our sins, wars have never been
lacking in this kingdom, and the natives*

*have been so molested and abused that
most of the people are gone from it*[376]
as their peace becomes war their land a grave

their villages empty of all they gave
in offerings to the seasons they served
2960   in their *tunkuy* time as nobody's slave

but of Sun and Moon and stars they observed
as time and order and map and cosmos
shattered by we *bearded idlers*[377]

eating and stealing whatever we found,[378]
*pillaging and burning and appearing
the example of complete cruelty.*[379]

2970   So it was that Pizarro sent the three –
Bueno, Zárate, Pedro de Moguer – to
strip Qorikancha of its destiny,

to tear Inti Sun from the path it flew
by winter and summer from dawn to dusk,
over lands once farmed where deserts now blow

through hollow stores strewn with broken husks
of memory parched where no *chasquis*[380] run
the Royal Roads binding present with pasts

we have melted to all we have stolen.
The land we garrotte like Atahualpa,
skinning an empire we parch in the Sun

whose goodness we have turned now to fire
that burns as we laugh at all we have done.
But *nor is it any use to discuss*

the ravages we commit in these lands.
In less than one month it seemed that all the
pestilence of the world had assailed it[381]

from the point of our swords, forcing to flee
the farmers the builders the courtiers,
whose lives we broke without shame or pity

though God has punished our men, and most
of these leaders have died miserably
in wretched deaths, a frightening thought to

serve as a warning,[382] a warning unheard
by the pirates who sacked Cajamarca[383]
in the grand shadow of the *kuntur* bird,

which glides on the wings of Viracocha

across the fading sky of a cosmos
whose last breath was wrenched from Atahualpa

3010   by such *cruel, bloodthirsty and vicious*
people,[384] my people, my *conquistadores*
with whom I now have the mountains to cross

as we burden the slaves, captive from wars
we alone made in the name of our lord –
greed, the hunger that is the food of our cause.

We eat all we find in Huamachuco,
and pass on through the valley of Jauja
3020   where the Indians fleeing towards Cuzco

were killed, *so that in many places*
one could see nothing but the profusion
of blood streaming from their wounds[385] as they ran,

leaving gold and many beautiful women
in the hands of the Marquis Pizarro, *in*
this miserable land because of our sins

3030   *evil men were never lacking*,[386] as the land
emptied of *many fine and beautiful herds*
which now are almost none where I stand

remembering how legendary words
spread the search for what they call El Dorado
which has cost many people so dearly[387]

from the hunger turning land to dust,
the stores from which Inca's people fed

3040   emptied as we feasting Spaniards passed

by roads along which Inca had once led
his millions through Illapa's thunderous
roar, to where now the *Pacha* people fled.

*

In the rocks and rivers and mountain skies,
between the fading stars of *Qoyllur*
where into thunder the *kuntur* flies,

that is there we Spaniards banished Inca,
3050   from the golden world we shipped in ingots
which ride the river to Seville,

where now in the year 1551
I stand on the banks of Guadalquivir,
a *cronista* bringing on his return

a truth I will tell without favour or fear,
that *many many times I have seen with my
own eyes these and other more severe*

3060
things done to these unfortunate people[388]
I watched disappear before my eyes.
How many have died it is not simple

to know, however much this *cronista* tries
to join *Inkarrí*[389] body with the head
we Spaniards severed when we stole the prize

of gold, then turned to dust the Royal Road,

3070   poisoned generous souls with our greed and sin,
     and enslaved the living to bear our load.

     So they died, from hunger not just within
     the fine men and women who once they'd been,
     but from that despair that came of knowing

     our mounted knights could not be beaten.
     So we stole their lives as we stole their souls
     and stole the harvest they would have eaten

3080

     when once the stores would have filled the bowls
     but which now our rampage has left empty.
     We hollowed this land and turned men to shells

     crushed beneath Santiago's cavalry[390]
     into the dust that is *Tahuantinsuyu*
     which only later became this story.

     Yes, only later could we see what hell
3090   we made for Inca and the millions there,
     Qorikancha torn by the Catholic bell

     that chimes of hours no life should bear.
     All was one, *tunkuy*, where the puma prowled
     by the curling banks of Vilcanota.

     All was one, where the raging waters coiled
     between *Uku*, *Kay* and *Hanan Pacha*.
     All one, where *Illapa* spoke and *kuntur* soared

3100

     where only now we know how many were
     killed: there were 9 million when we came,

little more than 600,000[391] there

within the hundred years our work was done
and Friar Valverde had ripped confession
from Atahualpa then cast the ragged sun

to San Domingo's baying dogs,[392]
which feast now on the bones of Qorikancha.
We killed the people when we killed their gods

and parched the terraced *cordillera*,
and now we wander through the ruin
we drained of lives whose cosmic ashlar

made sacred the bond of sun and rain
the Inca worked as terrace and stream
until our Day of Judgement came

and the pirate priest chimed Inca's scream
through the cloister where now the vaulted rose
fades by a sign that says 'keep off the stone',

in tongues that speak of *conquistadores*,
but whose name we learned with four centuries passed
is *cide genos*,[393] the *genocideurs*.

3110

3120

9: Gitarama

BY MAY 7 THE RWANDAN PATRIOTIC FRONT HAD ADVANCED TO THE PERIMETER AT ONE END OF KIGALI AIRPORT. THE AREA ON THE CITY SIDE OF THE AIRPORT, AS WELL AS THE KANOMBE BARRACKS, HAD BEEN DEPLETED OF TROOPS AS THE RPF ADVANCED. THE GOVERNMENT HAD MEANWHILE FLED TO A TOWN NEAR GITARAMA, THIRTY MILES SOUTH OF KIGALI. I DROVE WITH ANTHONY KABANO TO THE EDGE OF THE AIRPORT, AND REACHED A GROUP OF BUILDINGS ACROSS FROM WHICH WAS THE ROAD I KNEW LED INTO KIGALI. THE RPF POSITIONS, MARKED BY TRENCHES INTENDED TO PROTECT ITS TROOPS STATIONED IN THE CITY SINCE BEFORE THE CRISIS ERUPTED ON APRIL 6, WERE ALMOST WITHIN SIGHT. THE REMAINS OF THE GOVERNMENT ARMY WERE NOWHERE TO BE SEEN. IN THE FACE OF ANTHONY'S STIFF RESISTANCE, I TOLD HIM I WOULD CONTINUE INTO KIGALI, ACROSS A FRONT LINE WHICH IN FACT SEEMED NON-EXISTENT AND WHICH APPEARED APPARENTLY TO HAVE BEEN DESERTED. A GROUP OF JOURNALISTS THEN APPEARED FROM THE CITY. I KNEW THEM, AND WE DROVE TOGETHER UP THE HILL AWAY FROM THE AIRPORT, INTO THE SILENT,[394]

3130

3140

3150

empty,
　　　late

　　　　　afternoon

　　streets

　　　of Kigali
3160　*where now*
the poetic act changes
with the amount of background reality
embraced by the poet's consciousness.

In our century
that background is,
in my opinion,
related to the fragility of those things we call
civilization
3170　*or culture.*

What surrounds us,
here and now,
is not guaranteed. It could just as well not exist
—

so man constructs
poetry
out of
the remnants
3180　*found*
in
ruins.[395]

This

ruin.

This
is
3190   him.
Now
it
is
him.
This ruin.
This one.
Here.
Writing for you. Writing for you. This
one
3200   who
is
the fragility of those things
we
call.

We call.

We call
it
3210   a
name.
Though it does not exist.
This one. Writing for you. Writing for
you. This one
who
is
the fragility of those things
that pass now

in the one who tells:

3220 *When I walk I am asleep, when I sleep I am awake,*
I run, hunted and covered with sweat[396]

and drive, haunted, where the road is
wet
and dive gun hail where a trap is set.
I will be the ruin. There is nothing to be made
from my remnants,
here, where the Nyabarongo foams
through its gorge
and men *run, hunted and covered with*

3230 *sweat*
dew
mountain
rain
mist
hot
with
fear
where I will die
in a metal blaze

3240 which ignites the road.
I will die here
and never will I tell what *I see*[397]
and never will I tell what *I have seen.*[398]

What is it that I have seen?

What it is that I have seen

without becoming what I have seen?

3250 I am not what I have seen.
I am not being what I have seen.

It is not me.
I am not the one to whom Kajuga said:
You can get around everywhere.
We're going to help you circulate everywhere in the
country,
to see what has been going on,
to see what has happened[399]
because I will not become what I have
3260   seen.
I will not become the ruins.
What am I in this place?
What am I
to see what has been going on,
to see what has happened
where smoke from fires billows into damp air
where a smiling boy is selling bananas beside the road
near a man who has found the time to wash his car
while a woman walks past carrying a baby in one hand and an eight-inch
3270 blade in the other
where farmers work the hillside
where at Kamonyi a teenage boy with a three-foot sword in an animal-skin scabbard
is in charge of a group of boys
who are drinking beer
and have stick grenades
jammed inside their
belts.
And nothing happens.
And everything happens.
3280 And this is everything.
For being nothing.

It is nothing

When all has happened

The disemboweling

Of what is

3290

So it becomes

What is not

I saw all that is not

All that is not

All that is not

3300

Of being what it is

All that is not what it is.

Shall I tell you? What will you do if I tell you? What shall I
tell you? What can you hear me say?

Witness

3310

Who must tell you

Of all that is not

From within what became

By the roadside

At the roadside

3320   Where a woman walks
                                            past

                                                    carrying

                                                            a baby in one hand

                                                                    and an
                        eight-inch blade

3330   in the other
                        at the roadside
                        on the way
                        to Gitarama.

                                                    *

                        There.

                        There is a place. There is a place. It is a name. It is a name. A geography.
3340   On a map. Gitarama town. Muvambi village
                        Where
                                            a helicopter is parked on a football pitch

                                            surrounded by low wooden huts

                                            and grassy patches are crisscrossed with concrete paths

                                            and government officials come and go
3350

about the business

of genocide.

Here are those men,
    sitting behind desks,
        speaking on radios,
            giving orders,

3360   writing memoranda.

We have done everything we can to pacify the areas under our control. The massacres are now more or less over, and people are returning to work.[400]

Prime Minister Jean Kambanda is sweating as he lies

his truth his truth his truth his truth his truth his truth his truth his truth his truth his truth his

3370   truth

from the hollow of a bone mouth
the hollow heat of a wetted skull
spike spliced in the hunch of its gnarl.

There is no eye. There is no eye to glass the mirror. There is
no mirror. No mirror here.

No mirror here

3380

To look on down the way.

A hollow gaze follows up steps to a room where the Interim President is poised on a chair.

Here is the Interim President poised on a chair.

His front teeth are gold.

3390   He wears a three-piece suit.

He wears a large gold ring on a wrinkled finger.

He became Interim President when a missile destroyed the plane of the President he replaced.

The killing triggered the genocide.

He is in an Interim. Between some others. An Interim.
3400   Between the rivers of meat.

We have demanded that the population remains calm. We have condemned all the massacres. After the death of the President, there was a great shock among the population. There were confrontations on both sides. We will pursue the law.[401]

Interim President Theodore Sindikabwabo is a pediatrician.

Interim President Theodore Sindikabwabo is a *genocideur*
3410

poised on the chair in his office as he tells me

                we will pursue the law
                we will pursue the law

and so

the poetic act changes
with the amount of background reality
3420 *embraced by the poet's consciousness*

and so

in our century
that background is,
in my opinion,
related to the fragility of those things we call

civilization[402]
3430

I see now among my ashen totems
I see now in a gilded grin
I see within the leader's sanctum
the *Akazu* wraps its savage in,
  where the red-brick wall is so neatly laid
  and the garden flowers so carefully clipped,
  where what is done is what is said
  where a promise made is a promise kept
with honour told in a language spoken
3440 there in a room where the word is the noise
heard alone by the one who has broken
into the place where the womb now devours
  the bone and the flesh it may once have cradled,
  the pediatrician who sits there
  as man as man as man as man as man
  watching me through his spectacle stare,
 as I write down the words he spins in the air
 of that damp room where my witness falls blind

to truth and words and all the poet might find

3450 in the ruin

that
is
the
one
who
writes.
This ruin.
This one.
Here.

3460 Writing for you. Writing for
you. This one
who
is
the
one
you call.
You call
it
a

3470 name
though it does not exist.
This one. Writing for you.
Writing for you. This one
who
is

waiting to learn the name he became
waiting to be the word now written
waiting to learn all he has spoken
will never be silenced by the shame

3480 that is all the truth the witness is told
of how he watched as the killing time came

and how he saw spit then drip from the gold
of a mouth that spoke so calm and so tame
it seemed as human
as the words of Jean-Luc Mbarushinana
ARMS CROSSED TIGHT WHERE HE STOOD ON THE
RED EARTH, IN FRONT OF THE VIRGIN
IMMACULATA CATHOLIC MISSION IN KABGAYI,
ON THE OTHER SIDE OF GITARAMA, WHERE 15,000
TUTSIS WERE SHELTERING. "THEY HAVE COME
EVERY NIGHT," SAID JEAN-LUC, A TEENAGER.
"THEY LOOK FOR YOUNG PEOPLE, OR CIVILIZED,
EDUCATED PEOPLE, AND TAKE THEM OUTSIDE.
THE TEACHERS AND ADMINISTRATORS ARE THE
PEOPLE THEY WANT. AND THE STUDENTS. THEY
WANT THE PEOPLE WHO ARE INTELLIGENT, AND
DEMAND THEIR IDENTITY CARDS." HE FELL
SILENT AS A GENDARME STRODE OVER TO A
CROWD GATHERED AROUND A BOY, AGED 10,
WITH A SHORN HEAD AND STARVING FACE WHO
HAD A FIVE-INCH GASH ACROSS THE TOP OF HIS
HEAD. "IT HAPPENED YESTERDAY MORNING,"
WHISPERED A MAN, FELICIEN TWAGIRAMUNGU,
POINTING TO THE BOY WHOSE BEWILDERED
EYES WERE SET IN A FACE OF FEAR, AS THE
GENDARME WHO PERHAPS WOULD SOON KILL
HIM STOOD LISTENING NEARBY. "HE WENT TO
FIND WATER, BECAUSE THERE'S HARDLY ANY
HERE. HE SAW SOME MILITARY AND THEY
ATTACKED HIM. WE THOUGHT HE WAS DEAD,
BUT INSTEAD HE CAME BACK BADLY INJURED. IT
HAPPENED JUST OUTSIDE THE CHURCH." A
CROWD GATHERED AROUND US WHERE WE
TALKED. "HOW DO THE SOLDIERS OUTSIDE

TREAT YOU?" I ASKED. "THEY HAVE TAKEN
TWENTY-EIGHT PEOPLE AWAY FROM HERE, AT
NIGHT, IN THE PAST WEEK," SAID A WOMAN. "NO,
IT'S THIRTY PEOPLE NOW," SAID ANOTHER,[403]
      her fate known,
3520   the last days of all those there
              now drifting behind them,
                    me and some others their witness.

      Their witness.

      The hollow Being of witness.

      The hollow witness
who learns nothing
3530 and teaches nothing
because nothing is learned.
Because there is nothing to learn.
Because everything is known.
There is no surprise.
      Because in our beginning is our end,[404]
      as the womb devours
      the bone and the flesh
      it may once have cradled.

10. Cora-Berliner Straße 1

And

every line we succeed in publishing
today – no matter how uncertain the
future to which we entrust it – is a
victory wrenched from the powers of

darkness[405]

And when the sound of early hour chimes
Is not the time of telling what is told
And when the storyteller breaks his spell
On the hollow words wisdom cannot hold,

Then

totalitarian lawfulness,
defying legality and pretending
to establish the direct reign of justice
on earth, executes the law of History
or of Nature without translating it
into standards of right and wrong for
individual behavior. It
applies the law directly to mankind

without bothering with the behavior

of men[406]

who face all that is known with what is known
of a truth that is memorialised in stone
as truthful as the one who died alone
3570   to leave behind the story that has shown

death is the sanction of everything that
the storyteller can tell. He has borrowed
his authority from death[407]

as he – the I of the poem – pieces
all that may become what can be said
of a Being scrutinised as species
whose mystery is faked for those he led
3580

as

to say that the Holocaust is inexplicable,
in the last resort,
is to justify it,[408]

to justify,

in words that speak of how
3590

I understand that the whole of the
Holocaust mythology is,
after all,
open to doubt[409]

The holocaust of Germans in Dresden
really happened.
That of the Jews in the gas chambers of Auschwitz
is an invention[410]

3600

of the minds and hands of family men,
loyal citizens of utopia,
whose monstrous powers of captivation
shaped hatred from hysteria
>so many to this day are loving still,
>in the private darkness of a moment
>parched of the remembrancer's will
>to tell us where the people went,
and conjure from the hell that is their womb

3610

the *other side of history*[411] they must live
in pursuit of the darkness of the tomb
their gods preach is the light their angels give
>*to camouflage their goals.*
In an attempt to hide the fact that they are fascists and anti-Semites with a
specific ideological and political agenda, they state that their objective is to
uncover historical falsehoods, all historical falsehoods[412]
>so that what is known can then become unknown
>so that what is said is just what someone said
>so that knowing has no meaning

3620

>so that living has no truth
and all is debateable, one side and the other, so
any truth can be retold. Any fact can be recast. There is no ultimate historical reality.
Holocaust denial is part of this phenomenon[413]
>now shadowing the stelae
>where the sound of early chimes
>is the hour
>without number
>without time,

134

the timeless numberless hour

3630 that tolls

where all that is

crosses the path

of all that was.

But tell me one thing, and this is why I'm going to get tasteless with her,
because you've got to get tasteless, Mrs Altman, how much money have you
made out of that tattoo since 1945? [Laughter] How much money have you
coined for that bit of ink on your arm, which may indeed be real tattooed ink?
And I'll say this, half a million dollars, three quarters of a million for you
alone[414]

3640 so what is known can then become unknown

so what is said is just what someone said

so knowing has no meaning

so living has no truth

in the world remade

reshaped

revised

denied

by men with a mission to defy the *historical smother-out*[415]

which for them is *anything which emphasised national socialist savagery*[416]

3650 anything by which this *morbid interest was prolonged and stimulated*[417]

as they pursue their

threat to all who believe that knowledge and memory are among the keystones
of our civilization[418]

in its making and its burning

in the agony of its birth

in the un-Being of its death

3660 among the stelae now mourning

the mystery it may answer
of what is real and what is night
of what is made though out of sight
of the footsteps of the dancer

pacing a cosmos for something of the past
in search of all that remains of the future
in words the page of the poet cannot capture
3670   in rhyme nor reason
so *the tendency towards reversion*
may explain the powerful attraction
which totalitarian philosophy and practice can exert upon humanity.
Totalitarianism appeals to the desire to return to

the womb[419]

the devouring womb

3680   bearing and consuming, so it becomes *only by the struggle against*
constantly appearing false ideas that the truth is enlarged and clarified[420]

though the horror is of a kind
that the poet cannot capture
as he ponders on the culture
that no wisdom could define

with any more than the conclusion drawn
beside a dying grate just after dawn
3690   had broken through the fog that rubbed the panes
and *lingered upon the pools that stand in drains*[421]

where the answer lies not in what happened
but what took place when the curtain opened

onto the street below where footsteps pass
in pursuit of future goals borne of the past

spent

Trying to learn to use words, and every attempt
Is a wholly new start, and a different kind of failure[422]

we cannot believe
may be repeated

until again it happens

on the street below where our footsteps pass
in pursuit of goals borne of a past

from which we in our horror have learned only that

our sense of historical motion is no longer linear, but as of a spiral[423]

as we yearn a past our nightmares haunt
with words we mould from the times they echo
by the hollow of day the breakers taunt
in motion the motion no times now know
          as what was known *is now passing quickly out of*
          reach[424]
            truth now a darkness in search of light,
            where the birches are hushing in their grove
            and a sparrow perched on its bough takes flight
across ash meadows
          as your pastures move
              in the sunlit breeze
              that warms the wire

and shifts in dapple shade as shards
that catch a yellow butterfly in its short flutter of life
3730   passed upon the ashen memory of air
we breathe that is the breath of you.
> You, who are watching.
> You, who see my fear.
> You, who brought me here, and now watch me
> where I stand

beside the tracks,
waiting for you
as evening falls on broken walls
that will forever be the prison
3740   where you will cage us in your wire
where you will drag us to your gallows
where your name is ever written
in the ash your slaves have scraped
from the flames your angels stoke.
You are watching
from every shadow the stelae cast
the length of Cora-Berliner Straße,
whose truth
> is what is found
3750   not what is made[425]

of the bitter rampage of the beast
who is waiting on the street for that parade
he imagines once again as marching past
when the *un-blushing, oft-repeated swindle of the six million Jews gassed*[426]
has been exposed as *the frightful Jewish-Bolshevik manufacturing of atrocities*[427]
> he scrawls in pamphlets for like-minded folk,
> back-room clusters of exiled minds
> sweating bone ash from the fires they stoke
> with dreams of Führer, as they fasten the blinds

3760   to keep the truth of day far distant.

Truth,
which resists being projected, by whatever means, into the realm of
knowledge,[428]
which *does not enter into relationships, particularly intentional ones*[429]
with pasts
when there is no past
behind the
lock locked
no entry
3770   green door
which opens onto the cobbles
that clutch the come-and-go
of murmured recollections
in footsteps
shifting
forward
forward a little
into the past that has no past
where the step of steps on wooden steps
3780   is the living
who come to see
who is living among the dead
remembered in a smile captured by the glass
on which reflections
shuffle in a queue
of sightseers aiming to remember
the face they never knew

beside the canal

3790

where the ashen sun drifts,

and by way of land and water

makes memory of its shadow
where all that is
crosses the path
of all that lies beside
Cora-Berliner Straße,

        and the danger is that
3800   memory may be all
        or memory may be nothing
            in the symbol of the shadows cast.
            All or nothing. It is here or it is not,
            that truth may yet be knowledge
            when truth cannot be knowledge
            but is alone the truth
we choose to see in the shadow cast
we choose to know or not to know
we choose to believe of another past
3810   we choose to carry wherever we go.
            It is alone, the truth. It belongs to no one
in the room where Heidegger delivers testament
to the editor and ex-SS *Hauptsturmführer*,[430]
who together range a landscape without sentiment
like warriors who had never been to war.
        So what was it that you meant when it was you told your
        students
            Let not doctrines and ideas be the rules of your Being.
            The Führer, himself and he alone,
3820   *is today and for the future German actuality and its*
            law?[431]
And all these years later you reply that
            When I took over the rectorate
            it was clear to me
            that I would not get through it
            without making compromises[432]

that never occurred to Walter Benjamin,
as he struggled with that suitcase at Portbou,
and took his life on the coast of fascist Spain
to be free from his tormentor *Gestapo*
   so far from where his cousin Hannah Arendt
   saw all that once was life now turn to fear
   when all her mentor Heidegger once meant
   became the passing trains that disappear
to the east from where none would be returning
to the court of Freiburg's *hidden king*,[433]
as his pupil lover became a woman running
from the prize that was the reason of his Being
   for which she is now the one to be forgiving
   an old man, who sips *black milk of daybreak*[434]
   in the evening light when the orphan brings
   arnica as the *schmetterling* forsake
the meadow where burned-out gods were seeking
each to teach the other's private silence.
The Professor brought thought to life again,[435]
so she forgave him for his time of tyrants,
   Hannah, who heard the past's dead treasures speak
   through the *Sein und Zeit* the poet orphan
   Celan died every day of each new week,
   tortured, *mit den verfolgten in spätem*
un-verschwiegenem, strahlendem Bund.[436]
Heidegger *was still young enough to learn*,[437]
she would insist of the man she could not
condemn for the silence he offered in return.
   Nothing revisionist, nothing denied,
   while the *hidden king* lived the aftermath.
   Nothing to say, not a man horrified,
   as one who followed the Todtnauberg path
asked: *wessen Namen nahms auf vor dem meinen?*

3830
3840
3850

141

3860   *Whose name did the book register before*
           mine[438] became one now listed there among
           the shadows that drift in memory of the sun,
                       through ashen time traced
                       by those burning feet
                       that wait now at the corner
                       of that Berlin street?

Acknowledgments

Thank you to the following copyright holders for the permission they have granted to include extracts from the following works:

Adorno, Theodor: Excerpt from: *Theodor W. Adorno, Collected Works in 20 volumes. Volume 6: Negative Dialectics.* (E.B.Ashton, trans.) © Suhrkamp Verlag Frankfurt 1966. All rights reserved by and controlled through Suhrkamp Verlag Berlin. Used by the kind permission of Suhrkamp Verlag. Akçam, Taner: *A Shameful Act: The Armenian Genocide and the Question of Turkish Responsibility* (London: Constable, 2007, trans. by Paul Bessemer). Used by the kind permission of Little, Brown Book Group. Akçam, Taner: *Killing Orders: Talat Pasha's Telegrams and the Armenian Genocide* (Cham, Switzerland: Springer Nature/Palgrave Macmillan, 2018). Used by the kind permission of Springer Nature. Arendt, Hannah: *The Origins of Totalitarianism* (2017: London, Penguin Modern Classics). Used by the kind permission of Penguin Books. Barnes, Harry Elmer: 'Revisionism: A Key to Peace', in: *Revisionism: A Key to Peace and Other Essays* (San Francisco: Cato Institute, 1980). Used by the kind permission of Cato Institute. Bauer, Yehuda: *Rethinking the Holocaust* (New Haven & London: Yale University Press, 2001). Used by the kind permission of Yale University Press. Benjamin, Walter: Excerpt(s) from THE CORRESPONDENCE OF WALTER BENJAMIN AND GERSHOM SCHOLEM by Walter Benjamin, translation and introduction copyright ©1989 by Penguin Random House LLC. Used by the kind permission of Schocken Books, an imprint of the Knopf Doubleday Publishing Group, a division of Penguin Random House LLC. All rights reserved. Benjamin, Walter: *The Origin of German Tragic Drama* (London and New York: Verso, 1998) John Osborne (Trans.). Used by the kind permission of Verso Books. Celan, Paul: *Collected Prose*, (2003) Rosemarie Waldrop (Ed.) (Manchester: Fyfield Books/Carcanet Press Limited). Used by the kind permission of Carcanet Press Limited. Celan, Paul: excerpts from "The Straightening," translated by Michael Hamburger, from *Poems of Paul Celan*. Translation copyright © 1972, 1980, 1988, 1995 by Michael Hamburger. Reprinted with the permission of the publishers, Persea Books, Inc (New York), www.perseabooks.com. All rights reserved. Cesare, Donatella Ester Di: *Utopia of Understanding: Between Babel and Auschwitz*, Albany: State University of New York Press, 2012; (trans: Niall Keane). Used by the kind permission of State University of New York Press. Eichmann, Adolf: *False Gods* (2015) and *The Eichmann Tapes* (2015) (London: Black House Publishing Ltd). Used by the kind permission of Black House Publishing Ltd. Eliot, T.S.: *Collected Poems 1909-1962 by T.S. Eliot* (London: Faber and Faber Ltd, 1974). Used by the kind permission of Faber and Faber Ltd. Frankl, Viktor E: *Man's Search for*

Meaning, (London, Rider, 2011). Used by the kind permission of Penguin Random House. Hatzfeld, Jean: *Machete Season: The Killers in Rwanda Speak* (New York: Farrar Straus Giroux, 2005). Used by the kind permission of Profile Books. Heidegger, Martin: *Ponderings II-VI: Black Notebooks 1931-1938* (Richard Rojcewicz, trans.; Frankfurt: Klostermann GmbH, 2014). Used by the kind permission of Klostermann GmbH. Heidegger, Martin: 'The Thinker As Poet', *Poetry, Language, Thought* (New York: HarperPerennial, 2013; Albert Hostadter, trans.). Used by the kind permission of Harper Collins. Höss, Rudolf: *The Commandant of Auschwitz*, (London: Orion Publishing Group Ltd, 2000). Used by the kind permission of Orion Publishing Group Ltd. Kemal, Yaşar, *Look the Euphrates is flowing with blood: A history of the island - 1* (Altan Gokalp, trans.; Paris: Gallimard, 2004). Used by the kind permission of: The Marsh Agency. Lengyel, Olga: *Five Chimneys: A Woman Survivor's true story of Auschwitz*, (Chicago: First Academy, 1995). Used by the kind permission of Chicago Review Press. León, Pedro de Cieza de: *Pedro de Cieza de León: The Discovery and Conquest of Peru* (Durham & London: Duke University Press, 1998), Alexandra Parma Cook & Noble David Cook (Edited and Translated). Used by the kind permission of Duke University Press. León, Pedro de Cieza de: *The Incas of Pedro Cieza de Leon* (Harriet de Onis, trans.; Norman: University of Oklahoma Press, 1977). Used by the kind permission of University of Oklahoma Press. Lipstadt, Deborah: *Denying the Holocaust: The Growing Assault on Truth and Memory*: 78 words from Denying the Holocaust: The Growing Assault on Truth and Memory by Deborah Lipstadt Copyright © 1993 by The Vidal Sassoon International Center for the Study of Antisemitism, The Hebrew University of Jerusalem. McCarthy, Justin: *Turks and Armenians: Nationalism and Conflict in the Ottoman Empire* (Madison: Turko-Tatar Press, 2015). Used by the kind permission of Dr Justin McCarthy. Milosz, Czeslaw: THE WITNESS OF POETRY by Czeslaw Milosz, Cambridge, Mass., 1983: Harvard University Press, Copyright ©1983 by the President and Fellows of Harvard College. Müller, Filip: TITLE: *Eyewitness Auschwitz: Three Years in the Gas Chambers* ('the work') Filip Muller. Copyright © 1979. Used by the kind permission of Rowman & Littlefield Publishing Group. All rights reserved. Riggs, Henry H.: *Days of Tragedy in Armenia: Personal Experiences in Harpoot, 1915-1917* (Charlotte, NC: Gomidas Institute, 1997). Used by the kind permission of Gomidas Institute. Steiner, George: *In Bluebeard's Castle: Some Notes Towards a Re-definition of Culture* (London: Faber and Faber Ltd, 1971). Used by the kind permission of Faber and Faber Ltd. Steiner, George: *Language and Silence* (London: Faber and Faber Ltd, 1967). Used by the kind permission of Faber and Faber Ltd. Stewart, Susan: 'The Gigantic: Skywriting: Exteriority and Nature', in *On Longing*,

144

Notes:

Part One: Akazu

[1] Col.Theoneste Bagasora, *Chef de Cabinet*, Ministry of Defence, to MH, Kigali, Rwanda 13 April 1994.
[2] To MH, Rukara, 30 April, 1994.
[3] To MH, Gahini, 30 April, 1994.
[4] To MH, Nyarubuye, 27 April 1994
[5] To MH, Nyamata, 26 May, 1994.

Part Two: Prinzengracht 263

[6] Westerbork transit camp, 80 miles north of Amsterdam. 101,525 of the 107,000 Dutch Jews deported to Poland in 1942-44 were interned at Westerbork. Of those sent from there to Auschwitz-Birkenau and other death camps, more than 95,000 were gassed.
[7] The university to which Martin Heidegger was appointed Professor of Philosophy in 1928. His students included Hannah Arendt. Heidegger was elected rector of the University on 21 April 1933, and joined the National Socialist German Workers' ('Nazi') Party on 1 May 1933, remaining a member until 1945. In his inaugural address as rector on 27 May he expressed his support for Adolf Hitler, and in November 1933 signed the Loyalty Oath of German Professors to Adolf Hitler and the National Socialist State.

[8] Martin Heidegger, *Ponderings II-VI: Black Notebooks 1931-1938* (Richard Rojcewicz Trans., Bloomington: Indiana University Press, 2016), p.47

[9] 'Gleichschaltung' or Nazification of institutions, including universities under the Nazi regime.

[10] Hannah Arendt, 'Martin Heidegger at Eighty', *New York Review of Books*, 21 October 1971.

[11] Ibid.

[12] Martin Heidegger's most influential early work was *Sein und Zeit* – 'Being and Time' – published in 1927.

[13] Heidegger writes: "*National Socialism actually always already was there and has been prepared*". Martin Heidegger, *Ponderings II-VI: Black Notebooks 1931-1938* op.cit., p.103

[14] Heidegger writes: "*we want to provide the movement and its proper power, possibilities of world configuration and of development*". Ibid., p.98

[15] Friedrich Nietzsche, *Notebooks* (Summer 1886-Autumn 1887); https://plato.stanford.edu/entries/nietzsche-life-works/

[16] Prinsengracht 263, the house in which Anne Frank, her family and other Jews trapped in Amsterdam, hid in July 1942-August 1944.

[17] Donatella Ester Di Cesare, *Utopia of Understanding: Between Babel and Auschwitz*, (Keane, Niall, Trans., Albany: State University of New York Press, 2012), p.208

[18] On 24 July 1967 the poet Paul Celan visited Heidegger at Todtnauberg, the mountain village in which the philosopher had written his major works, including several of the 'Black Notebooks' in which he had first expressed support and later criticised the Nazis. Celan writes the poem 'Todtnauberg' following the visit. A radio play – 'Todtnauberg', by John Banville (https://archive.org/details/Todtnauberg_John_Banville) – is an account of Celan's visit.

[19] Paul Celan, 'Death Fugue', *Poems of Paul Celan*, (Michael Hamburger Trans., New York: Persea Books, 2002; revised and expanded), p.31

[20] Paul Celan, *The Meridian*, Speech on the occasion of receiving the Büchner Prize, Darmstadt, 22 October 1960. Celan explains that poetry may be an 'Atemwende', a 'turning of breath', when the poem that exists within the poet becomes the verbal expression of the poem, and is thereby communicated to the listener. *Paul Celan Collected Prose* (Rosemarie Waldrop Trans., Manchester, UK: Carcanet Press, 1986), p.37

[21] Paul Celan, *The Meridian*, Celan points out that poems can be seen to have their provenance in specific moments or dates. He refers on different occasions to the 'date' 20 January. In her study of Celan (op.cit), Donatella Ester Di Cesare identifies the dating as 20 January 1942 (p.192), the date of the Wannsee Conference, at which senior Nazis agreed on the 'Final Solution of the Jewish Problem'.

[22] Di Cesare, ibid., p.190

[23] Theodor W Adorno, *Theodor W. Adorno, Collected Works in 20 volumes. Volume 6: Negative Dialectics* (E.B.Ashton, trans.; New York: Continuum, 1973). Adorno's assessment that after Auschwitz "all culture is garbage" has been the most powerful argument that the Holocaust created the need for philosophers to reassess all that they had once held to be true of the human condition, pp.366-367

[24] Paul Celan, 'Conversation in the Mountains', *Paul Celan Collected Prose*, op.cit., p.17

[25] Paul Celan, 'Wolfsbean', *Poems of Paul Celan*, op.cit., p.341

[26] Paul Celan, 'Conversation in the Mountains', ibid., p.17

[27] Martin Heidegger, *Ponderings II-VI: Black Notebooks 1931-1938*, op.cit., p.75

[28] Ibid., p.80

[29] Ibid., p.80

[30] Ibid., p.42

[31] Ibid., p.80

[32] Heidegger writes: "*Der Stürm, the great experience and fortune that the Führer has awakened, literary existence at an end*". Ibid., p.81

[33] Heidegger writes of Nazism as embodying "*the new essence of truth*". Ibid., p.82

[34] George Steiner, *In Bluebeard's Castle: Some Notes Towards the Redefinition of Culture* (Yale: Yale University Press, 1971), pp.37-45; Steiner advances the powerful theory that the Holocaust was in substantial part an act of revenge by formerly polytheistic Western culture, on Jewish religious belief, which had been the first to identify a single deity.

[35] See note 33.

[36] Rudolf Höss, *Commandant of Auschwitz*, (London: Phoenix, 2000), p.47

[37] Heidegger writes of the "*plight*" of myths, op.cit., p.109

[38] Rudolf Höss, *Commandant of Auschwitz*, op.cit., p.165

[39] Ibid., p.66

[40] Ibid., p.47

[41] Ibid., p.58

[42] Adolf Eichmann, *False Gods: The Jerusalem Memoirs* (London: Black House, 2015), p.8

[43] T.S.Eliot, 'The Hollow Men', *Collected Poems 1909-1962* (London: Faber & Faber, 1974)., p.77

[44] Heidegger writes: "*Barbarity is a prerogative of cultured peoples*". *Ponderings VII-XI: Black Notebooks 1938-1939*, op.cit., p.219

[45] Heidegger writes: "*What is now happening is the ending of the history of the great beginning of Western humanity*". Ibid., p.75

[46] Heidegger writes of the Nazi "*pseudophilosophy*". Ibid., p.133

[47] Heidegger writes: "*Thunderous applause is today still the weakest proof of approval*". Ibid., p.151

[48] Heidegger writes: *"drawn off course by any temptation"*. Ibid., p.316

[49] Ibid., p.194

[50] Heidegger referred to having *"mistook and undervalued"*. Ibid., p.319

[51] Heidegger refers to the *"erroneous paths of folklore"*. Ibid., p.323

[52] Ibid., p.323

[53] Eichmann: *False Gods*, op.cit., p.48

[54] Ibid., p.234

Part Three: Tawantinsuyu

[55] Michael E Moseley, *The Incas and their Ancestors: The Archaeology of Peru* (London: Thames & Hudson, 2001, revised edition), p.72

[56] Susan Stewart, *On Longing: Narratives of the Miniature, the Gigantic, the Souvenir, the Collection*, (Durham and London: Duke University Press, 1993), p.71; the full passage is: 'Our most fundamental relation to the gigantic is articulated in our relation to landscape, our immediate and lived relation to nature as it 'surrounds' us. Our position here is the antithesis of our position in relation to the miniature; we are enveloped by the gigantic, surrounded by it, enclosed within its shadow. Whereas we know the miniature as a spatial whole or as temporal parts, we know the gigantic only partially. We move through the landscape; it does not move through us. This relation to the landscape is expressed most often through an abstract projection of the body upon the natural world. Consequently, both the miniature and the gigantic may be described through metaphors of containment – the miniature as contained, the gigantic as container.'

[57] Joyce Tyldesley, *Myths & Legends of Ancient Egypt* (London: Penguin Books, 2011), p.37

[58] Father Bernabé Cobo, *History of the Inca Empire* (Roland Hamilton Trans., Ed., Austin: University of Texas Press, 1979), p.108

[59] Ibid., p.104. Cobo writes of Manco Capac and three brothers and four sisters surviving the flood, and becoming the eight from whom all Incas are descended; Pedro Cieza de León, *The Kingdom of the Incas* (written: 1548-1550) (César Chacón Rosasco, Gretel Bardález Zambrano Eds., Carlota María Rosasco Belschak Trans., Cusco: Editorial Piki EIRL, 2011), p.21; the Inca creation myth tells of a great flood whose six survivors were the inhabitants who became the Incas.

[60] Father Bernabé Cobo, *History of the Inca Empire*, op.cit., p.103

[61] Cristóbal de Molina, *Relación de las fábulas y ritos de los incas* (*The Fables and Rites of the Incas*) (written: 1575-6) (Clements R Markham Trans., Ed., New York: Burt Franklin, 1873), p.10

[62] Pausanias, *Guide to Greece: 1. Central Greece*, Book X, Phokis, 6 (London: Penguin Books, 1979) p.419. The mythology of devastating floods after which humanity is reborn, is present in creation myths worldwide; the role of mountains in these myths is likewise a common theme.

[63] Ovid, *Metamorphosis*, Book I, 365-380 (Arthur Golding Trans., London: Penguin Books, 2002), p.41-45

[64] *The Epic of Gilgamesh*, Tablet XI, 142-143 (Andrew George Trans., London: Penguin Books, 1999), p.93

[65] Andrew James Hamilton, *Scale and the Incas* (Princeton & Oxford: Princeton University Press, 2018), p.122.

[66] Ibid., p.140

[67] *Camay* was the Inca practise of giving a "generative essence" to inanimate objects; objects that had been invested with *camay* by a *camayoc* were called *camascas*. Ibid., p.48-49

[68] Ibid.

[69] Cristóbal de Molina, *Relación de las fábulas y ritos de los incas*, op.cit. p.4

[70] Runa Simi – the Inca name for the Quechua language.

[71] Pedro Cieza de Leon, *The Kingdom of the Incas*, op.cit., p.69

[72] Cristóbal de Molina, *Relación de las fábulas y ritos de los incas*, op.cit., p.30; the Inca prayer to Viracocha, the Creator.

[73] 'Royal road', of which there were four centred on Cuzco, and others built by each Inca on inheriting the title, ibid., p.47

[74] 'Tawantinsuyu' or – as spelled by the Spanish – 'Tahuantinsuyo', the name given to their empire by the Incas; the name means 'the four united regions', each of whose corners met at Cusco.

[75] Andrew James Hamilton, op.cit., p.138

[76] Pedro de Cieza de León, *The Incas of Pedro de Cieza de León* (Harriet de Onis Trans., Victor W. von Hagen Ed., Norman: University of Oklahoma Press, 1959), p.111

[77] Ibid., p.94

[78] Ibid., p.97

[79] Ibid., p.90

[80] Ibid., p.178

[81] Ibid., p.318

[82] Andrew James Hamilton, op.cit., p.140

[83] Michael E Moseley, *The Incas and their Ancestors*, op.cit., p.81

[84] Pedro de Cieza de León, *The Incas of Pedro de Cieza de León*, op.cit., p.266

Part Four: Am Großen Wannsee 56–58

[85] Minutes of the Wannsee Conference held at Am Großen Wannsee 56–58 outside Berlin on 20 January 1942, at which 16 senior Nazi military and administrative figures finalised the plan for the extermination of the Jews of Europe. http://www.holocaustresearchproject.org/holoprelude/Wannsee/wanseeminutes.html

[86] Paul Celan, *Paul Celan Collected Prose* op.cit., p.37

[87] Ibid., p.37

[88] Adolf Eichmann, *The Eichmann Tapes*, op.cit., p.142-143

[89] Theodor W. Adorno, *Negative Dialectics* op. cit., p.369

[90] Minutes of the Wannsee Conference, op.cit.,

[91] Adolf Eichmann, *False Gods*, op.cit, p.95; Eichmann is referring in retrospect – and in his own defence – to the other 14 men who participated in the Wannsee Conference.

[92] Hannah Arendt, *Eichmann in Jerusalem: A Report on the Banality of Evil* (New York: Penguin Books, 2006), p.276

[93] Adolf Eichmann, *False Gods*, op.cit., p.119

[94] Heidegger writes: "*marvellously awakening volklich will*". Martin Heidegger, *Ponderings II-VI: Black Notebooks 1931-1938*, op.cit., p.80

[95] In this connection see: Elie Wiesel, *Night* (London: Penguin Classics, 2006), p.28

[96] Heidegger writes: "*penetrating the great darkness of the world*". Martin Heidegger, *Ponderings II-VI: Black Notebooks 1931-1938*, op.cit., p.80

[97] Heidegger writes: "*in order to thereby join back into the great beginning the most secret volklich mission of the Germans*". Ibid., p.80

[98] In this connection see: Elie Wiesel, *Night*, op.cit., p.viii

[99] Ibid., p.xv

[100] Primo Levi, *If This Is A Man*, (Stuart Woolf Trans., London: Abacus, 1987), p.17

[101] Ibid., p.18

[102] Adolf Eichmann, *The Eichmann Tapes*, op.cit., p 315

[103] Ibid., p.109

[104] Ibid., p.126

[105] Ibid., p.314

[106] In this connection see: Elie Wiesel: *Night*, (London: Penguin Classics, 2006), p.28

[107] Primo Levi, *The Drowned And The Saved*, (Raymond Rosenthal Trans., London: Abacus, 1989), p.62

[108] Ibid., p.64

Part Five: Inyenzi

[109] The phrase 'mythico-history' is that of the social scientist Liisa H Maalki, *Purity and Exile: Violence, Memory and National Cosmology among Hutu Refugees in Tanzania*, (Chicago and London: Chicago University Press, 1995); she writes, regarding Burundi, which was ruled as one with Rwanda until 1962: 'The issue of who were the original, primordial occupants of the land now known as Burundi was central to the Hutu claim to rightful moral and historical precedence over the Tutsi, and to the Hutu people's status as "the true members" of the primordial nation, the aboriginal homeland...[It] was very much a contemporary question concerning the "true essence" of the Burundian "nation" as it should be, and as it was, according to the mythico-history, prior to the arrival of the Tutsi "impostors" or "race of foreigners"...The exalted position of the Tutsi in Burundi, suggests the mythico-history was founded, not on divine or natural premises, but on deception and ill-gotten power.', p.28

[110] Charles Ntampaka, Sec.Gen., Rwandan Association of Jurists, to MH, Kigali, 10 January 1994.

[111] 'Homeland'

[112] Justin Mugenzi, Leader of the *Parti Liberale* and Minister of Commerce, to MH, Kigali, 10 January 1994

[113] 'Jeannette', in: Jean Hatzfeld, *Machete Season: The Killers in Rwanda Speak* (Linda Coverdale, trans; New York: Picador, 2005, English edition), p.210

[114] Janvier Afrika, military trainer of extremist group, to MH, Nairobi, 7 June 1994.

[115] Ibid.

[116] Robert Kajuga, President of the *Interahamwe* militia, to MH, Kigali, 13 May, 1994

[117] Janvier Afrika, op.cit.

[118] Justin Mugenzi, op.cit.

[119] John Hanning Speke, *Journal of the Discovery of the Source of the Nile*, (Mineola, New York: Dover Publications Inc, 1996. Originally published: Harper and Brothers, New York: 1868 & Edinburgh and London: 1863), p.241.

[120] Ibid., pp.241-242.

[121] Ibid.

[122] Gianni Vattimo, "Historie d'une virgule: Gadamer et les sense de l'être", *Revue Internationale de Philosophie 213, no.3* (2000), Donatella Ester Di Cesare: *Utopia of Understanding: Between Babel and Auschwitz*, op.cit., p.5

[123] Justin Mugenzi, op.cit.

[124] Lieutenant Wenceslas, Rwandan *Gendarmerie Nationale*, to MH, Kigali, 13 May, 1994

[125] President Pierre Buyoya of Burundi, to MH, Bujumbura, 29 March, 1995. Buyoya explained: 'An ideology of extermination exists among the extremists of the Hutu and Tutsi. In 1959, in Rwanda, there was extermination. It was that event in Rwanda that

created the fear among the Tutsis in Burundi. In 1972 there was a civil war here. It's necessary to eradicate the ideology of extermination. It's difficult for outsiders to understand. To eradicate that ideology is a question of political development. How can it develop in a balanced way? Secondly, how do you punish the people responsible for it?'

126 Charles Ntampaka, op.cit.

127 'Jean', Hatzfeld, op.cit., p.50

128 Catharine Newbury, *The Cohesion of Oppression: Clientship and Ethnicity in Rwanda, 1860-1960*, (New York and Chichester, West Sussex: Columbia University Press, 1988), p. 51.

129 Justin Mugenzi, op.cit.

130 Ibid.

131 "Tuutsi and Hutu became political labels; 'ethnicity', such as it was, came to assume a political importance, determining a person's life chances and relations with the authorities. With the establishment of European colonial rule in the country, ethnic categories came to be even more rigidly defined, while the disadvantages of being Hutu and the advantages of being Tuutsi increased significantly. Passing from one ethnic category to the other was not impossible, but over time it became exceedingly difficult and, consequently, very rare." Catherine Newbury, op.cit., p.52

132 Maj.Gen. Paul Kagame, to MH, Mulindi, Rwanda, 8 January 1994

133 Ibid.

134 Ibid.

Part Six: Chapaghjur

135 Yaşar Kemal, *Look, The Euphrates is Flowing with Blood* (Altan Gokalp, trans; Paris: Gallimard, 2004, French edition, published as: *Regarde donc l'Euphrate charrier le sang: Une histoire de l'île – 1*), originally published as: *Firat Suyu Kan Akiyor Baksana*, Istanbul, 1998)

136 Ibid., p.92

137 2013 film: *Eve Dönüş: Sarikamiş 1915*; Director: Alphan Eşeli; see: http://www.thelongwayhome-themovie.com/

138 Kemal, *Look, The Euphrates is Flowing with Blood*, op.cit., p.92

139 Ibid., p.92

140 Ibid., p.92

141 Justin McCarthy, *Turks and Armenians: Nationalism and Conflict in the Ottoman Empire* (Madison: Turko-Tatar Press, 2015), p.115. Despite their diplomatic presence across the Ottoman empire and the fact of German officers occupying several of the most senior positions in the Ottoman army, the German diplomatic communications make no reference to a "revolt" in Sivas province; see: Wolfgang Gust Ed., *The Armenian*

Genocide: Evidence from the German Foreign Office Archives, 1915-1916, (New York and Oxford: Berghahn Books, 2014), pp.59-65

[142] The American academic Justin McCarthy writes (ibid): 'The rebels had continued importing arms', p.113, though gives no details of where the weapons came from, how they were imported, nor what weaponry was seized; McCarthy goes on to write that: 'Although estimates of weapons found in the western Anatolian provinces were not given precisely in the records, there were caches in regions with significant Armenian populations', ibid, p.115; he does not include evidence of these weapons, nor detail for what precise purpose they had been intended.

[143] Justin McCarthy asserts (ibid.): 'More than 12,000 Armenian males of fighting age went to Russia from eastern Anatolia immediately before the war or in its first few months.', p.118, while other accounts explain that the majority of Armenians who joined the Russian army were those – or descendants of those – who had moved to Russia following the Ottoman massacres of Armenians instigated by Sultan Abdel Hamid in 1895 and 1896. McCarthy further states: 'Once again it was the Europeans who ensured that finance flowed to the rebels from Europe and America…Nothing stood in the way of transfers of funds to the rebels.', p.137. He does not provide evidence of this, while the US Consul in Harpoot Province at that time, Leslie A. Davis, provides considerable detail of the difficulty faced by Armenians requesting funds from family members abroad; see: Leslie A Davis, *The Slaughterhouse Province: An American Diplomat's Report on the Armenian Genocide, 1915-1917* (New Rochelle: Aristide D Caratzas, Publisher, 1989), p.57, p.97

[144] Ronald Grigor Suny, *They Can Live in the Desert, but Nowhere Else: A History of the Armenian Genocide* (Princeton: Princeton University Press, 2015), p.364

[145] Diplomatic cable from the German Administrator in Erzurum (Scheubner-Richter) to the German Ambassador in Constantinople (Wangenheim), in: Wolfgang Gust (Ed.), *The Armenian Genocide: Evidence from the German Foreign Office Archives, 1915-1916*, (New York and Oxford: Berghahn Books, 2014), available at: http://www.armenocide.net/armenocide/armgende.nsf/$$AllDocs/1915-05-15-DE-012

[146] Robert Morgenthau, *Ambassador Morgenthau's Story* (Amazon EU S.a.r.L.: 2018), p.8

[147] It was the view of Robert Morgenthau, US Ambassador to the Ottoman court in 1913-1916, that fear was the major influence on the Young Turk regime that orchestrated the Armenian Genocide; Morgenthau writes of Talaat Paşa, the Young Turk Interior Minister: "Talaat frankly admitted that fear – the motive, which, as I have said, is the one that chiefly inspires Turkish acts – was driving Turkey into a German alliance." Morgenthau, *Ambassador Morgenthau's Story*, op.cit., p.43

[148] Aurora Mardiganian, *Ravished Armenia* (Indo-European Publishing, 2014; first published in 1918 by Kingfield Press, New York), p.125

[149] Morgenthau, op.cit., p.106

[150] Ibid., p.106

[151] Ibid., p.102

[152] The German diplomatic Administrator in Erzurum (Scheubner-Richter) wrote on 15 May 1915 to the German Ambassador in Constantinople (Wangenheim) that '...the apparent cause of the troubles in Van is the arrest and murder of some Armenian public personalities, especially that of Mr. Ishkhan and the Armenian deputy of Van, Vramiam, who both enjoyed great respect within the Armenian community...the government should have known that through these actions they had finally caused the infuriation which had been brewing for a long time, but particularly since the beginning of the war, and which could only be suppressed by the leaders, to break out...In many spots weapons had been assembled for some time now – in the earlier stages for the purpose of self-defence only against an eventual massacre, but later also for the purpose of an armed uprising. That ongoing mistakes have been committed by the Turks in the handling of the Armenian question is known only too well by Your Excellency, and likewise that these mistakes were exploited by the Russians long before the outbreak of the war to achieve systematic incitement...With regard to the present situation here I would like to observe that a rebellion on the part of the Armenians in Erzurum and its surroundings is not expected, despite the negligible numbers of Turkish military forces in existence here. The Armenians living in areas near to the Russian border have long ago left their homelands; some of them fled to Russia where they are said to have joined the Russian troops – as was the case in Van – to fight against the Turks. Some of them came to Erzurum. Isolated incidents, such as armed resistance in the case of requisitions in far away villages, the killing of Turks who wanted Armenian girls and women handed over to them, or the cutting and sabotaging of telegraph and telephone lines, and espionage are not unusual phenomena during a war in border areas containing mixed populations'; available at: http://www.armenocide.net/armenocide/armgende.nsf/$$AllDocs/1915-05-15-DE-012

[153] Diplomatic cable from the German Administrator in Erzurum (Scheubner-Richter) to the German Ambassador in Constantinople (Wangenheim), in: Wolfgang Gust Ed., *The Armenian Genocide*, op.cit; available at: http://www.armenocide.net/armenocide/armgende.nsf/$$AllDocs/1915-05-15-DE-012

[154] Ibid: http://www.armenocide.net/armenocide/armgende.nsf/$$AllDocs/1915-04-15-DE-002

[155] Ibid: http://www.armenocide.net/armenocide/armgende.nsf/$$AllDocs/1915-04-27-DE-002

[156] Ibid: http://www.armenocide.net/armenocide/armgende.nsf/$$AllDocs/1915-06-29-DE-002

[157] Ibid: http://www.armenocide.net/armenocide/armgende.nsf/$$AllDocs/1915-03-26-DE-001

[158] McCarthy, *Turks and Armenians*, op.cit., p.119

[159] Diplomatic cable from the German Administrator in Erzurum (Scheubner-Richter) to the German Ambassador in Constantinople (Wangenheim), Wolfgang Gust, op.cit., at: http://www.armenocide.net/armenocide/armgende.nsf/$$AllDocs/1915-05-15-DE-012

[160] Ibid: http://www.armenocide.net/armenocide/armgende.nsf/$$AllDocs/1915-06-30-DE-001

[161] Ibid: http://www.armenocide.net/armenocide/armgende.nsf/$$AllDocs/1915-07-07-DE-001

[162] German Administrator in Erzurum (Scheubner-Richter) to the German Ambassador in Constantinople (Wangenheim), op.cit.

[163] Justin McCarthy, *Turks and Armenians*, op.cit., p.124

[164] Ibid., p.127. McCarthy further writes: 'The rebellion reached the city of Van on April 20, 1914', p.125. This appears to be an error, and should read 1915; either way, the suggestion that the rebellion began outside Van and then 'reached' the city, is a strange assertion, as other accounts do not refer to 'rebellion' outside the city, only in the city.

[165] Ibid., p.160

[166] Ibid., p.197

[167] Ibid., p.196

[168] Ibid., p.195

[169] Ibid., p.197

[170] Taner Akçam, *A Shameful Act: The Armenian Genocide and the Question of Turkish Responsibility* (Paul Bessemer Trans., London: Constable, 2007), p.164

[171] Ibid., p.165

[172] Cable of 29 September 1915 sent by Talaat Paşa to the Provincial Governor of Aleppo; the record of the cables sent to the Aleppo branch of the Interior Ministry's Directorate for Tribal & Immigrant Settlement (*İskan-ı Aşair ve Muhacirin Müdüriyeti*) was obtained by Naim Effendi, Secretary during the genocide in the Deportation Office (*Sevkiyat Müdürlüğü*) of the Aleppo branch. The full excerpt of this cable reads: 'It had previously been communicated that the government, by order of the *Cemiyet* (the Committee of the Ittihad), had decided to completely annihilate all Armenians living in Turkey. Those who oppose this command and decision cannot remain part of the official structure of the state. Without paying attention to women, child, [and] incompetent, no matter how tragic the methods of annihilation might be, without listening to feelings of conscience, their existence must be ended', Taner Akçam, *Killing Orders: Talat Pasha's Telegrams and the Armenian Genocide* (Cham, Switzerland: Springer Nature/Palgrave Macmillan, 2018), p.35

[173] Ibid., p.35

[174] Henry H Riggs, *Days of Tragedy in Armenia: Personal Experiences in Harpoot, 1915-1917* (Charlotte, NC: Gomidas Institute, 1997), p.81

[175] Rafael de Nogales Méndez (1879-1936) was a Venezuelan soldier serving in the Ottoman army; see: Ronald Grigor Suny, *They Can Live in the Desert, but Nowhere Else*, op.cit., p.258

[176] Ibid., p.293

[177] Taner Akçam, *A Shameful Act*, op.cit., p.166

[178] Wolfgang Gust Ed., op.cit; available at:
http://www.armenocide.net/armenocide/armgende.nsf/$$AllDocs/1915-06-17-DE-003

[179] Leslie A Davis, *The Slaughterhouse Province: An American Diplomat's Report on the Armenian Genocide, 1915-1917* (New Rochelle: Aristide D Caratzas, Publisher, 1989), p.90

[180] Ibid., p.59

[181] Ibid., p.83, and Henry H. Riggs, *Days of Tragedy in Armenia*, op.cit., p.152

[182] Ibid., p.87

[183] Taner Akçam, *A Shameful Act*, op.cit., p.181

[184] Henry H Riggs, *Days of Tragedy in Armenia*, op.cit., p.152

[185] Morgenthau, op.cit., p.119

[186] Morgenthau, op.cit., p.103

[187] Ahmet Rafik, Ottoman army officer, Taner Akçam, *A Shameful Act*, op.cit., p.130

[188] The three key figures in the Young Turk regime were Talaat Paşa (Interior Minister), Enver Paşa (War Minister), and Djemal Paşa (Navy Minister).

[189] Taner Akçam writes of the decision to instigate the 'deportation' of the Armenian population, that 'if past deportations had been a matter of Turkification they were now, according to the well-known intellectual Doğan Avcioğlu, tied to the issue of "continuing or not to exist as a state". This change had a direct effect on the ultimate decision to annihilate the Armenians.' Taner Akçam, *A Shameful Act*, op.cit., p.128

[190] Talaat Pasha to Morgenthau, Morgenthau, op.cit., p.118

[191] Aurora Mardiganian, *Ravished Armenia*, op.cit., p.11

[192] Ibid., p.18

[193] Ibid., p.18

[194] Ibid., p.22

[195] Ibid., p.26

[196] Ibid., p.41

[197] Ibid., p.57

[198] Ibid., p.107

[199] Friedrich Nietzsche, *Notebooks*, Summer 1886-Autumn 1887; op.cit.

[200] Hassan Fehmi Bey, nationalist parliamentarian, 1920, quoted in: Taner Akçam, *A Shameful Act*, op.cit., p.135

[201] Morgenthau, op.cit., p.110

[202] 26 November 2003

[203] Henry H. Riggs, *Days of Tragedy in Armenia*, op.cit., p.93

[204] The Government of Turkey's detailed assessment of the 'Events of 1915' is available here: http://www.mfa.gov.tr/controversy-between-turkey-and-armenia-about-the-events-of-1915.en.mfa

[205] Ibid.

[206] Ibid.

[207] Ibid.

[208] Taner Akçam, *The Young Turks' Crime against Humanity: The Armenian Genocide and the ethnic cleansing of the Ottoman Empire* (Princeton and Oxford: Princeton University Press, 2013), p.194

[209] http://www.mfa.gov.tr/controversy-between-turkey-and-armenia-about-the-events-of-1915.en.mfa

[210] Ibid.

[211] Adolf Hitler, to the Oberkommandierenden, Obersalzburg, 22 August 1939, in: Deutschen Nationalbibliotek, (Norderstedt: GRIN Verlag GmbH, 2007), available at: https://www.grin.com/document/76273

Part Seven: Ulica Ofiar Faszyzmu 12

[212] Igor Bartosik & Adam Willma, *A Conversation with Henryk Mandelbaum: I was at the Auschwitz crematorium*, (Bydgoszcz: Media Regionale Sp. z.o.o, 2009), p.44

[213] Ibid., p.44

[214] Ibid., p.45

[215] Ibid., p.62

[216] Ibid., p.89

[217] Filip Müller, *Eyewitness Auschwitz: Three Years in the Gas Chambers*, (Chicago; Ivan R Dee, 1979), p.38

[218] Ibid., p.98

[219] Ibid., p.100

[220] Ibid., p.99

[221] Minutes of the Wannsee Conference, 20 January 1942; *see*: https://www.ghwk.de/fileadmin/user_upload/pdf-wannsee/protokoll-januar1942.pdf

[222] George Steiner, 'The Long Life of the Metaphor: An Approach to the Shoah', *Encounter*, 1987, pp.55-61

[223] The phrase is George Steiner's, who explains: 'I am a remembrancer. At the heart of my work is an attempt to come after the Shoah, culturally, philosophically, in a literary sense: to be somewhere around with all the shadows and the ghosts and the ash, which are so enormous here…There should be a few impractical Jews left in the great shadow world of Europe who at least remember what the civilization here was', from 'Art of Criticism', *Paris Review*, in Christine D. Chatterley, *Disenchantment: George Steiner and the Meaning of Western Civilization after Auschwitz* (New York: Syracuse University Press, 2011), p.60

[224] Steiner, 'The Long Life of the Metaphor', op.cit., pp55-61

[225] Paul Celan, 'Psalm', George Steiner (Trans.), in 'The Long Life of the Metaphor: An Approach to the Shoah', *Encounter*, 1987, p. 55-61

[226] Paul Celan, 'Psalm', *Poems of Paul Celan* (Michael Hamburger Trans., New York: Persea Books, 2002), p.153

227 Paul Celan, 'Psalm', *Selected Poems and Prose of Paul Celan*, (John Felstiner Trans., New & London: W.W.Norton, 2001), in: George Steiner (Trans.), in 'The Long Life of the Metaphor: An Approach to the Shoah', *Encounter*, 1987, pp. 55-61

228 Steiner, 'The Long Life of the Metaphor', op.cit., pp.55-61

229 Paul Celan, 'Psalm', *Poems of Paul Celan* (New York: Persea Books, 2002; Michael Hamburger, trans.)

230 Steiner, 'The Long Life of the Metaphor', op.cit., pp.55-61

231 Ibid., pp.55-61

232 George Steiner, *Language and Silence: Essays 1958-1966* (London and Boston: Faber & Faber, 1985), p.173

233 Dante, *Inferno*, Canto XXXIII, line 55 (Mark Musa Trans., London: Penguin Books, 1984), p.372

234 In his memoir, the *Commandant of Auschwitz* (4 May 1940-November 1943, 8 May 1944-18 January 1945), Rudolf Höss writes: 'When I was thirteen years old, an incident occurred which I must regard as marking the first shattering of the religious beliefs to which I adhered so firmly. [Pushed a boy down the stairs in school; was punished; didn't tell his father' confessed to his confessor; confessor told his father] I had always been taught that the secrets of the sacred confessional were so inviolable that even the most serious offences there confided to the priest would never be revealed by him...My faith in the sacred priesthood had been destroyed and doubts began to arise in my mind for the first time. I no longer went to this priest for confession...In fact I went further, and gave up going to confession altogether, since I no longer regarded the priesthood as worthy of my trust...In my childish ignorance I earnestly beseeched our Heavenly Father to make allowances for the fact that I was no longer able to go to confession, and to forgive my sins which I then proceeded to enumerate. Thus did I believe that my sins had been forgiven me, and I went with trembling heart, uncertain as to the rightness of my actions, to communion in a church where I was unknown. Nothing happened! And I, poor, miserable worm, believed that god had heard my prayer, and had approved of what I had done. My spirit, which in matters of belief had up to then been so peacefully and surely shepherded, had been severely shaken and the deep, genuine faith of a child had been shattered.' Rudolf Höss, *Commandant of Auschwitz*, (London: Phoenix, 2000), p.34-35

235 Ibid., p.35

236 Dante, op.cit., lines 94-96, p.372

237 Steiner, 'The Long Life of the Metaphor', op.cit., pp.55-61

238 Rudolf Höss, op.cit, p.151

239 Ibid. p.152

240 Adolf Eichmann, *The Eichmann Tapes: My role in the Final Solution* (London: Black House, 2015), p.109

241 Revelation 20:13-15

242 Isaiah 24:21-22

[243] Filip Müller, *Eyewitness Auschwitz*, op.cit., p.130
[244] Rudolf Höss, *Commandant of Auschwitz*, op.cit., p.150
[245] Ibid., p.126
[246] Ibid., p.127
[247] Ibid., p.128
[248] Ibid., p.105
[249] Ibid., p.141
[250] Ibid., p.105
[251] Ibid., p.156
[252] Ibid., p.144
[253] Ibid., p.133
[254] Ibid., p.146
[255] Höss writes that captured Russian soldiers were brought to Auschwitz from a variety of locations; their murder by gassing in 1941 was the first use of the Zyklon B gas that would subsequently be used to murder Jews, gypsies and others at Auschwitz-Birkenau; Ibid., p.145-147
[256] Ibid., p.147
[257] Ibid., p.198
[258] Ibid., p.199
[259] Ibid., p.155
[260] Piotr Setkiewicz Ed., *The Private Lives of the Auschwitz SS* (William Brand Trans., Auschwitz-Birkenau State Museum, 2015), p.72
[261] Ibid., p.121
[262] Ibid., p.29
[263] Ibid., p.42
[264] Ibid., p.57
[265] Ibid., p.63
[266] Ibid., p.77
[267] In this connection see: Elie Wiesel, *Night* (London: Penguin Classics, 2006), p.29
[268] Ibid., p.29
[269] Piotr Setkiewicz Ed., *The Private Lives of the Auschwitz SS*, op.cit, p.102
[270] Olga Lengyel, *Five Chimneys: A Woman Survivor's True Story of Auschwitz* (Chicago: First Academy, 1995), p.225
[271] Ibid., p.42
[272] Ibid., p.94
[273] Ibid., p.108
[274] Ibid., p.123
[275] Viktor E. Frankl, *Man's Search for Meaning*, (London, Rider, 2011), p.24
[276] Ibid., p.62
[277] Ibid., p.60

278 Donatella Ester Di Cesare, *Utopia of Understanding: Between Babel and Auschwitz* (Niall Keane Trans., Albany: State University of New York Press, 2012), p.190

279 Ibid., p.190

280 Ibid., p.188

281 Ibid., p.188

282 Ibid., p.189

283 Ibid., p.192

284 Paul Celan, 'Death Fugue', *Poems of Paul Celan*, (Michael Hamburger Trans., New York: Persea Books, 2002; revised and expanded), p.32

285 George Steiner, *The Poetry of Thought: From Hellenism to Celan* (New York: New Directions Books, 2011), p.207

286 Paul Celan, 'Death Fugue', *Poems of Paul Celan*, op. cit., p.31

287 Paul Celan, 'The Straitening', ibid., p.115

288 Ibid., p.115

289 Ibid., p.115

290 In this connection see: Elie Wiesel, *Night*. op.cit., p.29

291 Celan, 'The Straitening', op.cit., p.115

292 Ibid., p.115

293 Ibid., p.115

294 Shlomo Venezia, *Inside the Gas Chambers: Eight months in the Sonderkommando of Auschwitz*, (Cambridge UK: Polity Press, 2009), p.57

295 Ibid., p.59

296 Höss, *Commandant of Auschwitz*, op.cit., p.151-152

297 Venezia, *Inside the Gas Chambers*, op. cit., p.59

298 Paul Celan, 'The Straitening', op.cit., p.115

299 Venezia, *Inside the Gas Chambers*, op.cit., p.155

300 Paul Celan, 'The Straitening', op.cit., p.115

301 In this connection see: Elie Wiesel, *Night*. op.cit., p.37

302 Paul Celan, 'The Straitening', op.cit., p.115

303 In this connection see: Elie Wiesel, *Night*. op.cit., p.33

304 Paul Celan, 'The Straitening', op.cit., p.115

305 In this connection see: Elie Wiesel, *Night*. op.cit., p.33

306 In this connection see: Ibid., p.37

307 Paul Celan, 'The Straitening', op.cit., p.115

308 In this connection see: Elie Wiesel, *Night*, op.cit., p.42

309 In this connection see: Ibid., p.91

310 In this connection see: Ibid., p.28

311 Paul Celan, 'The Straitening', op.cit., p.115

312 In this connection see: Elie Wiesel, *Night*, op.cit., p.37

313 In this connection see: Ibid., p.45

314 In this connection see: Ibid., p.37

[315] Paul Celan, 'The Straitening', op.cit., p.115

[316] Rudolf Höss, *Commandant of Auschwitz*, (London: Phoenix, 2000), p.150

[317] George Steiner, 'A Kind of Survivor' in *Language and Silence* (London: Faber & Faber, 1985), p.174

[318] In this connection see: Elie Wiesel, *Night*, op.cit., p.29

[319] In this connection see: Ibid., p.68

[320] George Steiner, op.cit., p.175

[321] In this connection see: Elie Wiesel, *Night*, op.cit., p.65

[322] Primo Levi, *If This Is A Man* (London: Abacus, 1987), p.16

[323] Piotr Setkiewicz Ed., *The Private Lives of the Auschwitz SS*, op.cit., p.111

[324] T.S.Eliot, 'The Waste Land', *Collected Poems* (London: Faber & Faber, 1974), p.55

[325] Primo Levi, *If This Is A Man*, op.cit., p.28

[326] Donatella Ester Di Cesare, *Utopia of Understanding* op. cit., p.192

[327] Primo Levi, *If This Is A Man*, op.cit., p.23

[328] Ibid.

[329] Ibid., p.46

[330] In this connection see: Elie Wiesel, *Night*, op.cit., p.42

[331] Paul Celan, 'The Straitening', op.cit., p.115

[332] In a devastating phrase, George Steiner writes: 'When a Jew opposes the parochial ferocity into which nationalism so easily (inevitably) degenerates, he is paying an old debt'; George Steiner, 'A Kind of Survivor' in *Language and Silence*, op.cit., p.177

[333] Rudolf Höss, *Commandant of Auschwitz*, op.cit., p.198

[334] Primo Levi, *If This Is A Man*, op.cit., p.137

[335] Ibid., p.129

[336] Piotr Setkiewicz Ed., *The Private Lives of the Auschwitz SS*, op.cit., p.111

[337] Miklós Nyiszli, *Auschwitz: A Doctor's Eyewitness Account* (London: Penguin Classics, 2012), p.38

[338] Ibid., p.129

[339] Ibid., p.30

[340] George Steiner, *Language and Silence: Essays 1958-1966* (London and Boston: Faber & Faber, 1985), p.173

[341] Miklós Nyiszli, *Auschwitz: A Doctor's Eyewitness Account*, op.cit., p.143

[342] Ibid., p.89

[343] Ibid., p.51

[344] Martin Heidegger, 'The Thinker As Poet', *Poetry, Language, Thought* (Albert Hostadter Trans., New York: Harper Perennial, 2013), p.4

[345] Ibid., p.9

[346] Heidegger writes: "*the marvellously awakening volklich will is penetrating the great darkness of the world*". Martin Heidegger, *Ponderings II-VI: Black Notebooks 1931-1938*, op.cit., p.80

[347] Heidegger writes: "*great experience and fortune that the Führer has awakened a new actuality, giving our thinking the correct course and impetus*". Ibid., p.81

[348] Martin Heidegger, 'The Thinker As Poet', op.cit., p.10

[349] Heidegger writes: *"the aim of showing that völkisch Being is the goal of the people – is that then an aim at all and not rather its destruction"*. Martin Heidegger, *Ponderings VII-XI: Black Notebooks 1938-1939*, op.cit., p.233

[350] Sophocles, *Antigone* lines 408-409 (Robert Fagles, Trans., London: Penguin Books, 1984), p.77

[351] Ibid., lines 413-416, p.77

[352] Martin Heidegger, interview with *Der Spiegel*, conducted by Rudolf Augstein and Georg Wolff, 23 September 1966; published May 31 1976; see http://lacan.com/heidespie.html#_ftnref9

[353] George Steiner, *The Poetry of Thought: From Steiner to Celan* (New York: New Directions, 2011), p.211

[354] Paul Celan, 'Todtnauberg', op.cit., p.281

[355] Paul Celan, 'The Straitening', ibid., p.115

[356] Theodor W. Adorno, *Negative Dialectics*, (New York: Continuum, 1973), p.362

[357] Ibid., p.362

[358] Ibid., p.371

[359] Primo Levi, *If This Is A Man*, op.cit., p.46

[360] Theodor W. Adorno, *Negative Dialectics*, op.cit., p.362

[361] Ibid., p.362

[362] Paul Celan, 'Death Fugue', *Poems of Paul Celan*, op. cit., p.31

[363] Martin Heidegger, 'The Thinker As Poet', *Poetry, Language, Thought*, op.cit., p.9

[364] Theodor W. Adorno, *Can One Live After Auschwitz?* (Rolf Tiedemann Ed., Stanford: Stanford University Press, 2003), p.71

[365] Ibid., p.78

Part Eight: El Dorado

[366] Alonso Manrique de Lara y Solís, Grand Inquisitor (1523-31), a native of Badajoz in the region wherein Pedro de Cieza de León was born in 1520, where he was Bishop in 1499-1516. MH notes

[367] The port on the Gulf of Cadiz where ships from the New World would moor before sailing upriver to Seville. MH notes

[368] The Roman road linking Llerena with Seville. MH notes

[369] Captain Pedro de Heredia had been the first Spaniard to land at Cartagena, in January 1533. MH notes

[370] Sebastián de Belalcázar (sometimes spelled Benalcázar) was one of the early conquistadors to have accompanied Francisco Pizarro. Pedro de Cieza de León, *The Incas of Pedro de Cieza de León* (Harriet de Onis Trans., Victor W. von Hagen Ed., Norman: University of Oklahoma Press, 1959), p.xliv

[371] *rumi chaca* literally, 'stone' and 'bridge' in Quechua, recognised as the northern-most point of the Inca empire. MH notes

[372] Pedro de Cieza de León arrived in the Inca kingdom on 18 April 1547, 12 years after his arrival in the New World; 'Tahuantinsuyu' was the Spanish spelling of Tawantinsuyo. MH notes

[373] De las Casas evoked the writings of St Isidore of Seville, by emphasising that the Greek word 'historein' meant one who 'sees' or 'knows'; Bartolomé de las Casas, *A Short Account of the Destruction of the Indies*, (Nigel Griffin Trans., London: Penguin books, 1992) from the Introduction by Anthony Pagden, p.xxxv

[374] De las Casas' account of Benelcázar's burning of the Indian lords in Quito was provided to him by a Franciscan friar, Marcos de Niza, who witnessed the slaughter. Ibid., p.111

[375] Pedro de Cieza de León, *The Incas of Pedro de Cieza de León*, op.cit., p.lxiii

[376] Pedro de Cieza de León, *The Discovery and Conquest of Peru* (Alexandra Parma Cook & Noble David Cook Eds. and Trans., Durham & London: Duke University Press, 1998), p.267

[377] Ibid., p.187

[378] Ibid., p.187

[379] Ibid., p.205

[380] The *chasquis* were couriers who ran in relays along the Royal Roads, carrying messages on behalf of the Inca and the administration; see Pedro de Cieza de León: *The Incas of Pedro de Cieza de León*, op.cit., p.46, p.63

[381] Pedro de Cieza de León, *The Discovery and Conquest of Peru*, op.cit., p.234

[382] Ibid., p.245

[383] Having paid the ransom of a room full of gold and silver, Atahualpa was murdered in Cajamarca on Saturday 26 July 1533. MH notes

[384] Pedro de Cieza de León, *The Discovery and Conquest of Peru*, op.cit., p.259

[385] Ibid., p.285

[386] Ibid., p.354

[387] Ibid., p.392

[388] Ibid., p.430

[389] Evolving in many versions throughout different communities in the Peruvian Andes, the *Inkarri* myth portrays the Spanish conquest as having severed the Inca's body from its head, with the reconnecting of the two bringing to an end the period of darkness precipitated by the European invasion; Alberto Flores Galindo, *In Search of an Inca: Identity and Utopia in the Andes* (New York and Cambridge UK: Cambridge University Press, 2010) p.7-8

[390] A statue in Cuzco's Cathedral depicts a bearded Saint James – Santiago – in the attire of a conquistador riding a white horse, beneath which – appearing to support the animal – is a cowering Inca. MH notes

[391] The demographer and writer Noble David Cook estimates that in 1530 – prior to the arrival of the conquistadors – the population of Peru was around nine million, and that by 1620 the Indian population stood at 601,645; Noble David Cook, *Demographic Collapse: Indian Peru, 1502-1620* (Cambridge: Cambridge University Press, 1981), p.114

[392] The Dominican order, of which Vicente Valverde – the priest who had accompanied Pizarro to Peru and who extracted conversion and confession from Atahualpa before witnessing his murder and burning – was a member, became the first Bishop of Cuzco; Valverde was responsible for the destruction of the Qorikancha and the construction of the current convent on its site. The Dominicans – named after Saint Dominic – were also known as the 'Hounds of God', or *Domini canes*. MH notes

[393] The term 'genocide', derived from the ancient Greek word *genos* (race or tribe) and the Latin *cide* (killing), was created by the lawyer Raphaël Lemkin, an advisor to the Nuremberg Trial chief counsel Robert H. Jackson; Raphaël Lemkin, *Axis Rule in Occupied Europe: Laws of Occupation, Analysis of Government, Proposals for Redress* (Clark, New Jersey: The Law Book Exchange LTD, & The Carnegie Endowment for International Peace, Second Edition, 2008), p.79

Part Nine: Gitarama

[394] Mark Huband, *The Skull Beneath the Skin: Africa after the Cold War* (Boulder: Westview Press, 2001), p.201

[395] Czeslaw Milosz, 'Ruins and Poetry' in *The Witness of Poetry* (Cambridge and London: Harvard University Press, 1983), p.97

[396] Czeslaw Milosz, 'Song of a Citizen': https://modernpoetryintranslation.com/poem/song-of-a-citizen%E2%80%A8/

[397] Ibid.

[398] Ibid.

[399] Robert Kajuga, interview with MH, Kigali, 13 May, 1994.

[400] Jean Kambanda, Prime Minister of the Rwandan interim government, interview with MH, Muvambi, Rwanda, 15 May 1994.

[401] Theodore Sindikabwabo, Rwandan interim president, interview with MH, Muvambi, 15 May, 1994.

[402] Czeslaw Milosz, 'Ruins and Poetry', op.cit.

[403] Mark Huband, *The Skull Beneath the Skin: Africa after the Cold War*, op.cit., p.201

Part Ten: Cora-Berliner Straße 1

[404] T.S.Eliot, 'The Four Quartets: East Coker' in T.S.Eliot, *Collected Poems 1909-1962* (London: Faber & Faber, 1974), 'In my beginning is my end.' p.184

[405] Walter Benjamin, letter to Gershom Shalom: *The Correspondence of Walter Benjamin and Gershom Shalom 1932-1940* (Gershom Shalom Ed., Cambridge, Mass.: Harvard University Press, 1992), letter dated January 11, 1940, p.262

[406] Hannah Arendt, *The Origins of Totalitarianism* (London: Penguin Books, 1951), p.607

[407] Walter Benjamin, 'The Storyteller: Reflections on the Works of Nikolai Leskov', at http://ada.evergreen.edu/~arunc/texts/frankfurt/storyteller.pdf

[408] Yehuda Bauer, *Rethinking the Holocaust* (New Haven & London: Yale University Press, 2001), p.38

[409] Judgement in the case: Irving v. Penguin Books Limited, Deborah E. Lipstadt [2000] EWHC QB 115 (11th April, 2000): Evidence from the official record: David Irving, section 8. 17; http://www.bailii.org/ew/cases/EWHC/QB/2000/115.html#6

[410] Speech by Irving, Dresden, 13 February 1990; ibid.

[411] The phrase is that of Deborah Lipstadt, who fought a successful defence against the accusation that she had defamed the historian David Irving (see: http://www.bailii.org/ew/cases/EWHC/QB/2000/115.html#6); Deborah Lipstadt, *Denying the Holocaust: The Growing Assault on Truth and Memory* (London: Penguin Books, 2016 edition), p.3

[412] Ibid., p.4

[413] Ibid., p.23

[414] Judgement in the case: Irving v. Penguin Books Limited, Deborah E. Lipstadt [2000] EWHC QB 115 (11th April, 2000): Evidence from the official record: David Irving, section 8. 17; http://www.bailii.org/ew/cases/EWHC/QB/2000/115.html#6

[415] The phrase is that of the revisionist historian Harry Elmer Barnes; Harry Elmer Barnes, 'Revisionism: A Key to Peace', in *Revisionism: A Key to Peace and Other Essays* (San Francisco: Cato Institute, 1980), p.64

[416] Ibid., p.64

[417] Ibid., p.64

[418] Lipstadt, op. cit., p.23

[419] T.S.Eliot, *Notes towards the Definition of Culture* (London: Faber & Faber, 1948, 1962), p.68

[420] Ibid., p.82

[421] T.S.Eliot, 'The Love Song of J Alfred Prufrock', *T.S.Eliot, Collected Poems 1909-1962* (London: Faber & Faber, 1974), p.3.

[422] T.S.Eliot, 'East Coker', op.cit., p.184

[423] George Steiner, *In Bluebeard's Castle: Some Notes Towards the Redefinition of Culture* (Yale: Yale University Press, 1971), p.69

[424] Ibid., p.99

[425] Lipstadt, op.cit., p.30

[426] Austin J. App, *A Straight Look At The Third Reich: Hitler and National Socialism: How Right? How Wrong?* (Takoma Park, Maryland: Boniface Press, 1974), p.17

[427] Ibid.

[428] Walter Benjamin, *The Origin of German Tragic Drama* (John Osborne Trans., London and New York: Verso, 1998), p.35

[429] Ibid., p.35

[430] Georg Wolff, an editor at *Der Spiegel* magazine, who – along with Rudolf Augstein – in 1966 conducted a lengthy interview with Heidegger, including some discussion of his past in the Nazi Party, which was published after Heidegger's death, on 30 May 1976: http://www.ditext.com/heidegger/interview.html; Wolf had himself served as an officer in the SS during World War Two.

[431] Ibid.

[432] Ibid.

[433] In her assessment of 'Martin Heidegger at Eighty' – published in the *New York Review of Books* on 21 October 1971 – Hannah Arendt wrote of her former Professor: 'For in Heidegger's case there was nothing tangible on which his fame could have been based, nothing written, save for notes taken at his lectures which circulated among students everywhere. These lectures dealt with texts that were generally familiar; they contained no doctrine that could have been learned, reproduced, and handed on. There was hardly more than a name, but the name travelled all over Germany like the rumor of the hidden king.' Hannah Arendt, Albert Hofstadter Trans., *New York Review of Books*, 21 October 1971; https://www.nybooks.com/articles/1971/10/21/martin-heidegger-at-eighty/

[434] Paul Celan, 'Death Fugue', *Poems of Paul Celan*, (Michael Hamburger, trans., New York: Persea Books, 2002; revised and expanded), p.31

[435] Hannah Arendt, 'Martin Heidegger at Eighty', op.cit., *New York Review of Books*, 21 October 1971; https://www.nybooks.com/articles/1971/10/21/martin-heidegger-at-eighty/

[436] Paul Celan: *'Mit den verfolgten in spätem, un-verschwiegenem, strahlendem Bund'* ('Pledged to the persecuted, by a late, un-tacit, luminous bond'); in *Atemwende* (1967), *Poems of Paul Celan*, op.cit., p.209

[437] Arendt, 'Martin Heidegger at Eighty', op.cit.

[438] Paul Celan, 'Todtnauberg': *'wessen Namen nahms auf vor dem meinen?'* ('whose name did the book register before mine?'), *Poems of Paul Celan*, op.cit., p.281